SITE WORK

D1438278

SITE WORK

ARCHITECTURE IN PHOTOGRAPHY SINC

ARLY MODERNISM

THE PHOTOGRAPHERS' GALLERY, LONDON

Published to coincide with the exhibition SITE WORK:
Architecture in Photography since early Modernism, selected
by Martin Caiger-Smith.

The Photographers' Gallery, London
12 July - 14 September 1991

Impressions Gallery, York
October - November 1991

Ikon Gallery, Birmingham
11 January - 15 February 1992

Cambridge Darkroom and the Eastern Region Centre for
Architecture Gallery
5 June - 18 July 1992

Edited by Martin Caiger-Smith and David Chandler

Designed by John Critchley and Neville Brody

Printed by Jackson Wilson, Leeds

SITE WORK is sponsored by
The Building Centre Trust

ISBN 0 907879 29 2

While The Photographers' Gallery gratefully acknowledges
financial assistance from The Arts Council of Great Britain,
the London Boroughs Grants Committee and Westminster
City Council, nearly fifty per cent of its income is generated
through book and fine print sales, donations and business
sponsorship.

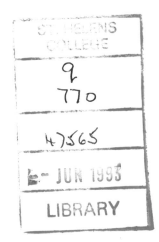

CONTENTS

FOREWORD

It must be every new Director's dream to inherit a project as pioneering, rich, enjoyable, provocative and enticing as this one. Unfortunately, I can take little credit for it as, like many of the best things in life, it has been a considerable time in the making. My gratitude therefore goes to Martin Caiger-Smith, until recently the Gallery's Exhibitions Organiser, who selected the exhibition, and his successor, David Chandler, for ensuring that this project came to fruition upon my arrival.

I took great care in choosing my opening adjectives, as they also describe the Gallery's future programme. This exhibition pushes ajar a number of cross-cultural doors; it is my intention to throw them wide open. With the help of practitioners from many areas, we intend to enlarge the perception of photography and its central place in all our lives.

Whatever your background, I believe you will find much to enjoy in the guided tour of the relationships between photography and architecture which unfolds over the next 96 pages – led by our distinguished contributors. The fact that they can approach their subject from such diverse corners, and so generously – even riotously – shed light on some of the landmarks in their individual journeys, makes this catalogue an exceptional document.

If only all cultural walls would so convincingly tumble whenever the clarion trumpet blows!

My last important and enjoyable duty is to thank the numerous specialists, photographers and others who have given so generously of their time, support and advice:

Janet Abrams
Robert Elwall, *Royal Institute of British Architects, London*
Ian Jeffrey
Peter Greenaway
Ken Jacobson
Mr Von Lint, *Factory Van Nelle, Rotterdam*
Bob Mann and Jerry Marshall, *fotomann inc, New York*
Alexandra Wettstein, *Marlborough Graphics, London*
Jonathan Bayer
Ute Eskildsen, *Museum Folkwang, Essen*

John T. Hill, *Connecticut*
Debra Cohen, *Life, New York*
Carolyn A. Davis, *George Arents Research Library, New York*
Peter Hahn, *Bauhaus Archive, Berlin*
Dr Herman Moeshart, *University of Leiden*
Mary Drugan, *New York*
Esto Photographics, *New York*
Arcaid, *London*
Ronald J. Hill, *New York*
Cornelia Regner-Hörl, *Frankfurt*
Professor Margaret Harker
Andrew Mead, *Architectural Press, London*
Kay Roberts, *Actualites, London*
John Leslie, *Museum of Modern Art, Oxford*
Farideh Cadot, *Paris*
Bernard Millet, *Marseille*
Eileen Hale, *Los Angeles*
Larry A. Viskochil, *Chicago*
Stuart Smith
Nick England
Hester von Royen
Linda Wilhelm, *Houston*
Marie-Agnès Benoit, *Montréal*
Wendy Wood, *New York*
Priska Dissel, *Galerie Rudolf Kicken, Cologne*
Superchrome Services Limited
Fletcher Priest, Architects

Sue Grayson Ford
Director

PREFACE

Site Work aims to reflect various aspects of the complex interrelations between architecture and photography. The one exists around and about us in the real world, large-scale, three-dimensional, the other presents an image and a reduction of that reality on the flat plane. Yet both, in formal terms, could be said to be about the play of light as it articulates form, space and surface. Both can be assigned a purely functional role, and both can aspire to the status of art. Architecture, and the contemporary urban environment, has always been a central subject for photography; and our experience of architecture is reliant to an extraordinary degree on the mediation of the photographic image, used and reproduced in a vast array of contexts.

The exhibition is wide-ranging and open-ended, rather than comprehensive, for the field is vast. It does not offer a photographic account of twentieth century architecture. The criteria for assessing work have been photographic rather than architectural. *Site Work* brings together many of the great, as well as some lesser known photographers of architecture, whose interests have embraced equally the landmarks of architectural history and the anonymous, the vernacular, and the ruin...

Site Work draws on independent photography and art practice and also on 'functional' images of the architectural press and profession – areas often held apart – to represent a range of approach as broad as the use of the photographic medium itself. It breaks dividing lines to highlight an interlocking of concerns and cross-fertilisation of ideas, and to emphasise the basic truth (acknowledged broadly for the first time in this modernist period) that photography, however used, cannot be neutral, an objective science. Every photograph of a building presents a viewpoint refracted by issues of style and aesthetics just as much as by the basic formal problems faced by all – the translation of the four-dimensional experience of three-dimensional forms (here, buildings) in the real world onto the still, two-dimensional plane of the photograph.

The exhibition focuses on reactions to contemporary architecture, and opens at the point of photography's enthusiastic reception of the modern city and of the New Architecture in the first decades of the century, the heroic years of early modernism. It branches out from there to follow particular lines up until the present day: the presentation and denial of architectural space; the building in its urban environment; the picturing of architecture as a process; photography 'at the service of architecture'; and architecture as a pretext for art.

The essay which follows, *Site Work*, explores some of these formal concerns and wider issues which thread their way through the show, while Robert Elwall's provides a context for the section on British architectural photography as employed by the profession and the architectural press. The other essays extend the debate beyond the scope of the exhibition. Ian Jeffrey examines pre-war literary as well as visual attitudes to the metropolis, the view from the margins as much as from the vanguard; Janet Abrams looks into the phenomenon of the photographic image on the global circuit in architectural practice and criticism, while Peter Greenaway, finally, lays bare his personal obsessions with the image of architecture in film.

I am grateful to them all for their contributions, and also to Robert Elwall for advice on British architectural photography and to Janet Abrams for useful discussions throughout. I would also like to thank those who have given help and advice at all stages of the project, particularly Richard Pare, Mark Haworth-Booth, Pam Roberts, Andrew Mead, Ute Eskildsen, Tom Evans, Kay Roberts of Actualites, Mike Wells, Richard Ehrlich, Val Williams, Lynne and Richard Bryant of Arcaid, Simon Esterson and Tim Street-Porter. Finally, I am grateful to Frances Morris for constant help; and to the staff of The Photographers' Gallery, especially to Rachael McLanaghan and Ruth Charity, and to David Chandler, who took on the task of organising the exhibition in its later stages.

Martin Caiger-Smith

5

Frederick Evans, 'A Sea of Steps', Wells Cathedral, 1903

SITE WORK MARTIN CAIGER-SMITH

'Space begins because we look away from where we are...' writes Gus Blaisdell (in an essay on the work of the American photographer Lewis Baltz).[1] Architecture is first and foremost about space, and what we see of it depends on where we stand, and how we look.

In his influential 1893 essay 'Problem of Form',[2] the German sculptor Adolf Hildebrand distinguished between two ways of seeing: pure vision, with the eye and body in rest, receiving a single, sharp and unified planar impression of a form, a 'distant image'; and its opposite, kinetic vision, with the body and eyes moving, approaching, circling or entering the object surveyed, and gaining a three-dimensional impression of the object. Hildebrand separated actual form – form as it is – from perceptual form – form as it is seen. The latter, of most interest to art and aesthetics he believed, involves time and motion, and depends on variable factors: illumination, environment and the viewpoint of the beholder.

The application of his theory to photography of architecture is clear. Every image places itself on a line between the extremes of distance and involvement, reflecting the rival dictates of description and sensation, the provision of data and the conveying of an experience.

Two classic turn-of-the-century images by Frederick H. Evans of Lincoln Cathedral could serve to illustrate Hildebrand's extremes. The first (a) is a distant image, presenting the entire face of the building over the rooftops of the town. The building appears frozen and spectral, more plane than volume, with a fine tracery of surface detail. The second (b), within a turret of the cathedral, is a tightly cropped view, a rhythmic interplay of space and form which offers an acute sense of presence, of moving through the building, with the stone of stairs and wall welling up hard against the plane of the photograph...

Architecture is experienced in four dimensions, it is appreciated and inhabited at the same time; the still photograph can only remain a window on that reality. Or, as curator John Szarkowski put it: 'a photograph can be about a building; it cannot be one'.[3] 'The

a Frederick Evans, *Lincoln Cathedral from the Castle, 1898*

photographer's problem' wrote Paul Strand in 1917, 'is to see clearly the limitations and at the same time the potential qualities of his medium'.[4] The picturing of architecture by photography this century has involved a constant testing of photography's limitations, an exploitation of its specific possibilities as well as a probing of its boundaries.

Whether regarding architecture as a site and sign of human presence and endeavour, or as pure abstract form, every photographer and artist using the medium has confronted these tensions: between the simple, flat photograph and the spatial complexities of architecture; between the photograph as document and as abstraction; between the static, single image and the depiction of architecture as a process; between the photographic 'framing' of a fragment and the wider view (or the building and its environment); and between the photograph as a transparent 'window on reality' and as an autonomous object with its own presence, occupying its own space.

These are questions which came to the fore early in the century, when Strand and others were defining a modernist approach to the medium, and as photography was moving beyond a largely neutral and subservient

b Frederick Evans, *Stairway in South West Turret, Lincoln Cathedral, 1898*

function as 'faithful record' of its architectural subject, to take on an interpretive role, assuming a relationship of mutual influence. And these concerns went hand in hand with an enthusiasm for what was new in architecture. In New York in those early years, photographers produced strong expressive responses (whether in a modernist or a lingering pictorialist mode) to the drama of the new high-rise city landmarks. In Coburn's *Broadway* of 1909/10 (plate 7) and Steichen's 1906 *Flatiron Building* (plate 6) space and mass evaporate in the Whistlerian dusk; particular detail gives way to looming profile and atmosphere. Strand's own famous *Wall Street* of 1915 is a masterly, highly charged reduction of its subject to an image of basic form revealed by light...

In Europe in the 20s, the urge to abstraction in photography was in harmony with developments in avantgarde architecture and art. A recent writer voices a commonly held view: 'With the translation of Bauhaus canon to

International Style, photography and architecture enjoyed a new fusion. Their coalescence was pure. The camera had little problem recording architecture as abstraction, simply because much International Style architecture was itself abstract'.[5] Photography shared ideas with architecture rather than merely recording its every facet. Werner Mantz's *Kölnische Zeitung* (plate 20) building by night, so redolent of the period, is all facade, a rigid symmetry enlivened by strong graphic illumination. Mantz's *Stairwell* (c) records no details, but distributes pure form and receding space in the manner of an abstract painting – compare for example a Josef Albers *Homage to the Square*...

Stairs and ladders were, in fact, a recurring motif in this period, of movement, dynamism, verticality. The New Photography of the 1920s (which filtered through to a photographic orthodoxy in the avantgarde architectural magazines of the 20s and 30s) proclaimed a new freedom of viewpoint, an empathy and a close engagement with its architectural subjects. Photographers sought the revelatory detail and the unfamiliar angle – technically

d Beaumont Newhall, *Chase National Bank, New York, 1928*

'true' perspectives confound and confuse expectations as the photographs strove to capture 'what the human eye does not see'.[6] Gravity is defied, and soaring diagonals proliferate, from Moholy Nagy's aerial abstractions (plate 17) to the architect Erich Mendelsohn's shots in his book *Amerika: An Architect's Picturebook* of 1927,[7] with his craning pedestrian's 'worm's eye' views from the street of multi-storeyed Manhattan as a towering architectural stage almost devoid of people. Such a vision reached the vertiginous extremes of Beaumont Newhall's *Chase National Bank* (d), and was further developed through superimposition and montage (a technique deriving from artistic practice which became central to professional architectural imagery), from the repeated reality of Hugo Schmölz's *Hotel Disch AG.* (plate 25) to the fiction of an *Untitled Landscape* by Thurman Rotan (plate 27), or Paul Citroen's photo-collage *Metropolis* (plate 28), a conflation of a multitude of architectural forms and spaces on the single picture plane. And at a time when architects and artists were inspired by futuristic notions of space/time, Hildebrand's ideas on the perception of space were developed, underpinning much theorising in photography and in architecture – and nowhere more so than by Moholy Nagy, as in his book *Vision in Motion* of 1946.

Surface Readings

An apparent opposite to this kaleidoscopic complexity is the concentration on facade, a vision of architecture as planar – a vivid and recurring theme in American imagery. Walker Evans's *Storefront, Moundville, Alabama* of 1936 (plate 41) is a stark, frontal rendition of humble American vernacular, leagues away from the photographer's own consciously

e Walker Evans, *Furniture Sign, near Birmingham, Alabama, 1936*

avantgarde studies of Brooklyn Bridge in 1929 (plate 12) or from what he had come to view as the 'artiness' of Stieglitz's followers and of the New Photography.[8] Evans's image appears a simple document – yet even here, formal strategies prevail. His long lens flattens space, and tight framing eliminates background, locking facade to picture plane. His photographs of wayside billboards (e) echo this treatment – pictures of architecture doubly reduced to the plane by innocent signpainter and knowing photographer alike.

They bring to mind a Diane Arbus photograph of 1963, *House on a Hill, Hollywood*,[9] which gives the lie to a building that seems to come from an Edward Hopper painting... Arbus's camera takes a sidestage view, exposing the structure as a flimsy sham, a film set flat – an appropriate metaphor for its location, perhaps, but also a telling indication of photography's complicity in erecting, and keeping up, this facade.

In part this interest in the facade took its cue

c Werner Mantz, *Stairwell, 1928*

from the architecture itself. A whole run of images – Eggleston's *Greenwood Moose Lodge* (f) is a fine example – lights on buildings constructed expressly for the frontal view, of those who pass by. West Coast artist Ed Ruscha made a bookwork in 1966, *Every*

f William Eggleston, *Greenwood Moose Lodge, 1981* (original in colour)

Building on the Sunset Strip (1966), as one long linear unfolding photograph to be viewed as if from a car, *en passant*. The book proved a strong influence on photojournalists; and this photographic way of seeing even finds its way into architectural theory and debate, in such publications as Peter Blake's tirade on the despoilation of the American landscape, *God's Own Junkyard*,[10] and Venturi and Scott Brown's *Learning from Las Vegas*,[11] an argument against the 'tyranny of space' in architecture, and a case for an architecture of broad-ranging imagery and allusion, for the building as self-evident sign, yielding to the viewer a clear external message of its function or contents...

The facades in Lewis Baltz's *New Industrial Parks near Irvine, California* (1974-5) (plates 42,43) by contrast, reveal little or nothing. Baltz's rendering of these anonymous factories and warehouses is impenetrable, flat in both senses, a meticulous 'document' which gives us no idea of what lies beyond, or within. Here surface – the facade alone – is the subject, rigorously organised in a fifty-one part series of images of recurring elements and spare, abstract motifs, showing evident formal and conceptual links with minimalist art of the time. The work represents only one stage in Baltz's sustained exploration of architecture and its spaces, in uncertain states of becoming or decay, meticulously observed yet always on the edge of abstraction.

Harry Callahan's photographs of high rise facades (plate 44), a preoccupation of his from the 50s to the 70s, also suggest an interest in minimalism, yet are less fixed, less easily read than Baltz's. 'Pictures of unoriented folding planes, in which positive and negative spaces oscillate ambiguously',[12] they reveal Callahan's Bauhaus inheritance, through Moholy Nagy's reformed Institute of Design in Chicago. They show a fascination with the possibilities of superimposition and multiplying of space, seen also in his many shop window images, where surfaces no longer block the view but lead through to, or reflect, other surfaces...

Peripheral vision

'...You cannot photograph New York without buildings. But I focussed on the *city*, not buildings.' (Berenice Abbott)[13]

The city is inseparable from a photographic consideration of contemporary architecture. The appearance and reception of a building, as photography proves, has much to do with its immediate surroundings. Unlike the splendid isolation of the drawing board, the building in the photograph is placed firmly within its environment.

William Clift, commissioned[14] to photograph the Old County Courthouse in St. Louis (g), finds his subject framed in reflection by the starkly contrasting new Equitable Building opposite, and draws together a century's architectural change on the one facade. Joel Meyerowitz, commissioned[15] in 1980 to commemmorate St. Louis's famous Arch (by Eero Saarinen) (plate 30), stalks the streets to survey his towering prey from every angle, in every context from the sublime to the banal. One image pictures the arch in far, shining splendour beneath a lowering sky; for the next, he sets his back to it to capture its reflection in the front window of the dingy Arch View Cafe.

g William Clift, *Reflection, Old St Louis County Courthouse, Missouri, 1976*

In his recent work in China in 1989 (plate 31), Olivo Barbieri adopts Meyerowitz's emotive register, heightening the drama of abandoned urban space by forcing together foreground and distance – forging a link between the intimate incidental signs of human presence, the scribble and clutter of signage of the quartière, and the unassailable, pulsating sublime of the collosi beyond. The contrast is especially striking, even surreal, in this setting of exotic vernacular, an abandoned stage caught by the long exposure at night. Barbieri sets small-scale disrepair poignantly against sleek ultramodern in a treatment which combines a tourist's wonder and a documentarist's eye for the inconsequential with a knowing play on the codes of commercial architectural photography (as epitomised, perhaps, by Richard Bryant, plate 37).

Bob Thall's work in Chicago in the early 80s (plate 45;h) displays a more all-consuming interest in spatial ambiguity. They seem to pick up some of Callahan's interests, on a wider, urban stage. Thall eschews any human resonance, picturing the bare terrain of the inner city wilderness in construction. His images recall the formal and conventional rules of landscape imagery only to subvert

h Bob Thall, *Chicago 1987*

them; his precise angles of view and unnatural alignments refuse a seemly progression from foreground to back, collapsing space and creating disjunctive uncertainties of form and scale.

The character of urban-industrial space is exhaustively explored by Gabriele Basilico (plates 46-49), through photographs which act as fragments of a whole, building a cumulative picture of a northern maritime port. His images combine the universal structures of industry – crane, coldstore, conveyer and chimney – with a distinctive northern French vernacular, playing graphic detail against stark, looming geometric form.

Photographers like Meyerowitz, Barbieri and Basilico work in a clearly subjective mode, conveying a developed response to a particular locale. Others impose a more rigid conceptual schema on their images, moving by a series of rigorous denials and preordained procedures to a declared position of unemotive 'objectivity'. Their streets are not the packed stage of the documentary street photographer: Axel Hütte, for example, sees his works (plates 56,57;i) as 'not primarily documentary photographs, but rather abstract spatial situations. All clues to everyday functions or consumerism are missing...'.[16] Hütte's architectural subjects are unremarkable in themselves, interstitial realms in states of transformation, and his interest in a dense, layered image is as much sculptural as concerned with the complexities of the urban environment it depicts. Thomas Struth, who worked together with Hütte in the 70s, also favours the 'objective' view from the navel, the systematic repetition of viewpoint in the central perspective of the empty urban thoroughfare, and the cumulative, atemporal evidence of 'anonymous architecture'. His urban images[17] represent a 'gigantic archive of contradictory architectural facts'[18] brought together from Tokyo, Düsseldorf,

i Axel Hütte, *London 1982-84*

9

Edinburgh...The individual images gain meaning in series, as Struth admits, in the 'interaction between one photograph and another, according to their similarities and differences'.[19]

Hütte and Struth both studied under Bernd and Hilla Becher (plate 58), whose work represents perhaps the most uncompromising stance in this direction, the photographic survey at its most reductive and programmatic. Their project over recent decades has been to document the 'anonymous sculptures' (blast furnaces, gas tanks, cooling towers) which are the now increasingly redundant architectural forms of disappearing primary industry. These far-flung constructions are shown in a cool, detached, analytical manner, and brought together as if embalmed, out of time and out of place, as a comparative anatomy in the reconstituted space of the multiple work, the book, or the exhibition installation...

Work in Progress

The American Ezra Stoller, doyen of the architectural photography profession in the postwar decades, proclaimed: 'the building that can be shown completely in one picture is not worth bothering about'.[20] A true description, he believed, could only be conveyed in a series of images. Such a view was of course not new – it had led in the 1850s to the masterly portrayal in photographic series of French cathedrals by Edouard Baldus or of Chartres in particular by Henri Le Secq . The influential American curator John Szarkowski went further: 'Architecture is not only a collection of buildings, it is a process', he wrote in 1959; '...photography of architecture should be less preoccupied with the finished building – an object – and more interested in the human and technical processes which precede and produce it'.[21]

Photography of work in progress is usually the preserve of the architect, engineer or developer, a functional record. But some photographers have exploited the aesthetic

j Berenice Abbott, *Foundations of the Rockefeller Centre,1930s*

appeal and the unclad all-revealing honesty of the unfinished structure. Lewis Hine celebrated the rise of the Empire State Building in 1931 as a triumph of anonymous human endeavour (plate 50); and Berenice Abbott's photographs (plate 51;j) of the New York Rockefeller Center in the same years show the massive building from the piles up, a view from within and below of an organic structure in the process of growing, its inner workings revealed.

Fifty years on, John Davies (plate 52), taking

k Catherine Wagner, *Eastern vista, George Moscone Convention Center Site, San Francisco, 1981*

up these themes,[22] seeks again for Hine's human angle, and an inside, nuts and bolts imagery to set against the pitiless pace and seamless cladding of the high-tech, prefabricated commercial development of today. Catherine Wagner's work (plate 5;(k) in San Francisco in the 80s lays bare the geometry and poetic order of structural elements. Static images capture moments, but combine in series to suggest a narrative, the passing of time... Wagner's *Wonderwall, Louisiana World Exposition* (plate 54) of 1984[23] shows the exhibition site after 'completion': a cornucopia of architectural elements and motifs designed in conscious quotation of historic precedents, to rival and recall P.H. Delamotte's well-known images of the Crystal Palace from the 1850s (plate 3). Even here, Wagner's pictures convey impermanence: she disdains the viewpoint from which the theatrical ensemble coheres, and instead goes backstage to view it as a temporary and fragile construct, put up at speed and soon, probably, to disappear. Wagner's Louisiana images (like those of Delamotte) 'admit an ambiguity as to whether the subject is under construction or in ruin...'.[24] The fragility of the temporary structure is conveyed also in Ryuji Miyamoto's *Pavilion of Tsukuba, Expo '85* (l). The pavilion's innards are exposed, its vulnerability emphasised – it is a contemporary ruin. Miyamoto's images of modern ruins take us beyond the facade again, within the buildings to share the pathos of their abandonment (plate 55). His photographs, 'fragments of fragments' as architect Isozaki comments,[25] are a telling indication of the photograph's capacity to 'outlive' monumental architecture. Photography caught the Crystal Palace's last moments in flames in the 1930s,[26] has witnessed the fall of the city planners' dreams as high rise housing developments are brought crashing down, and even the collapse of a city itself (as in the silent, compacted images of blasted and shelled Beirut

l Ryuji Miyamoto, *Pavilion of Tsukuba, Expo '85, Tsukuba, 1985*

appartment blocks, a testimony by the French photographer Sophie Ristelhueber).[27] Photography outlasts architecture, documents its construction, plots its mutations and records its decay in the present, preserving its presence for the future – as did Atget's intense photographic documents of disappearing old Paris early this century (plate 4), August Sander's images of prewar Cologne[28] and, in their way, the Bechers' continuing memorials to the increasingly defunct architecture of the industrial age.

Framing space

Architecture as subject, or as pretext? There is no simple antithesis to propose between the objective, documentary photograph and the conceptual or abstract photowork – where, for example, would the Bechers or Hütte be placed? Many artists using photography today, though, stress the autonomy of their work, its independence and essential difference from the architecture on which it is based. Despite their diverse aims, they all make clear the ways in which photography transfigures its subject, making of the architecture a new space, another, distinct reality.

Jan Dibbets provides an object lesson in such tactics. Since the 60s he has set the mechanical properties and monocular vision of the camera before the architectural subject, in a series of systematic explorations arising from a minimalist and conceptual background, from his early schematic excercises, his *Perspective Corrections,* to his more recent encounters with distinctive classical, Baroque and modern structures (plate 34). He analyses optics and perception, highlighting the process by which 'an illusion becomes an abstraction'. Dibbets makes clear that the form on the surface of the photograph is not that of the form photographed. His use of photography is abstract: 'He does not select an image from an existing sequence. The image he makes has not been seen before. It exists only as an image and has no model in the real world'.[29]

Julia Wood (plate 59), similarly, emphasises the frame as the ordering device of photographic space, an 'intervention' in reality. Her works[30] take glimpsed details of buildings in London's East End; their trapezoidal format disturbs and questions our usual easy acceptance of the conventional frame as a neutral form. The scored and painted squares on the works' surface, an overlay at odds with the facets of the buildings, set up a clear tension between the subjects portrayed and the work, suggesting a meeting of two perspectives, two illusions, the painterly and the photographic...

Georges Rousse (plate 33), unites abstraction and illusion on the picture plane, working in abandoned spaces and further developing Dibbets's *Perspective Corrections* to create new forms inscribed on the existing surfaces of the space which coalesce as three-dimensional 'structures' from one single viewpoint – the camera's. His is a private performance for the camera in a closed and forbidden location, which draws on the atmospheric charge and the character of the location for its resonance... Barbara Kasten's performance operates on another register, at the opposite pole to Rousse's meditations. Her *Architectural Site* works (plate 32) take on recognised contemporary public architecture

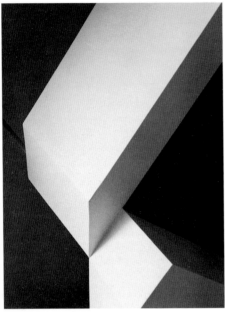

m Judith Turner, *Peter Eisenman House ,Thom loft, New York, 1989*

(such as the new art museums in America designed by Gehry or Isozaki) and transform, distort and abstract their forms, recasting them in saturated colour – a technically arduous ritual involving a support team and the full array of equipment and manipulative techniques.

Elsewhere, the line between collaboration and interpretive critique is more finely drawn. Judith Turner has worked at length on the architecture of such as Graves, Meier and Hejduk in America (plate 61;m). Her tightly cropped images resemble abstract compositions, yet they render space and explore interplay of forms in a manner which parallels the architects' intent even though they do not reveal 'information' about the buildings' detail or layout. Hélène Binet, too (plate 60;n), sees no distinction between 'professional' and 'art' practice, between her own aims as an artist and the dictates of the architectural project. Binet works closely with 'experimental' architects like John Hejduk and Daniel Libeskind who respond well to such symbiosis. Her images, like Turner's, do not claim to provide the 'whole picture'; they 'resemble architectural sections rather than plans'[31] and highlight the act of framing, presenting not a conventional 'detail', a complete rendering of constituent elements, but fragments of the whole – fragments which do not intend to 'abstract'.

Photography interpreting architecture can produce art which criticises as well as supports. Gordon Matta-Clark (plate 35) saw his performance/sculptures of the 60s and 70s as a 'dialogue between art and architecture'. His work involved, as he put it, 'undoing architecture', physically cutting into and breaking through the surface and layers of existing buildings to reveal their interiors, as a critical act of intrusion and liberation from enclosure, to redefine both the form and the function of the building. His political aims were matched by strong aesthetic considerations,

n Hélène Binet, *The House Without Walls by Daniel Libeskind, Milan Triennale, 1986*

however, and his use of photography of necessity (to preserve the temporary and the site-specific works for a wider audience) led him increasingly to play to the camera, to seek the revealing angle and viewpoint, to experiment with colour and multiple and sequential imagery.

Ottmar Hörl, working now, is in partnership with two architects,[32] and his photoworks act as a contribution to their combined theoretical stance. His multiple work *Die Grosse Vertikale II* (plate 62) – images of an anonymous high rise facade in Frankfurt caught in series by a camera falling from its top – forms part of a statement against dominant urban-architectural approaches based on the facade and outmoded perceptions of static space and linear time. The contrast between the pre-ordained clarity of the concept (the artist records the duration and distance of fall) and the 'arbitrary' nature of the resulting images is an appropriate end note...the camera's spiralling free fall through the architecture it depicts, suggests an infinity of new directions, and acts as a potent image of the possibilities and problems to be faced in this complex relationship between photograph and building.

Footnotes

1 Gus Blaisdell, writing on Lewis Baltz's 'Candlestick Point', in Lewis Baltz, *Rule Without Exception*, Des Moines, Iowa, 1990

2 Problem of Form, New York, 1902 (English translation); cited in C. van de Ven, *Space in Architecture*, Assen, 1987

3 John Szarkowski, 'Photographing Architecture', *Art in America*, summer 1959

4 *Seven Arts 2*, August 1917

5 Akiko Busch,*The Photography of Architecture: Twelve Views*, New York, 1987

6 Ossip Brik, in 'What The Eye Does Not See', 1926, trans. in Christopher Phillips ed., *Photography in the Modern Era*, New York, 1989

7 Erich Mendelsohn, *America: An Architect's Picturebook*, Berlin, 1926

8 see Jerry L. Thompson, *Walker Evans at Work*, London, 1983

9 reproduced in *Diane Arbus*, New York, 1972 (an Aperture monograph)

10 Peter Blake, *God's Own Junkyard: The planned deterioration of America's landscape*, New York, 1964

11 Robert Venturi, Denise Scott Brown and Steven Izenour,

Learning from Las Vegas: The Forgotten Symbolism of Architectural Form, MIT, 1977

12 John Szarkowski, *Callahan*, Aperture/Museum of Modern Art, New York, 1976

13 in an interview with Margarette Mitchell, 20/1/81, *Archetype*, II, II, spring 1981

14 as part of the national County Courthouse Project in the 1970s, by Joseph E. Seagram Inc.

15 the commission was from the St Louis Art Museum in 1977

16 Axel Hutte, from an interview reproduced in *Camera Austria*, 27. 1988

17 reproduced in *Thomas Struth, Unconscious Places*, Cologne, 1987

18 Ulrich Loock, 'Photos of the Metropolis', ibid.

19 Thomas Struth, ibid.

20 Ezra Stoller, 'Photography and the Language of Architecture', *Perspecta 8*

21 Szarkowski, op. cit.

22 Davies was commissioned by Davenport Associates to

photograph the Broadgate development in the City of London from 1989-91

23 a commission by the Canadian Centre for Architecture, Montreal

24 Drexel Turner, in Catherine Wagner, *Changing Places*, Rice University, Texas, 1988

25 Arata Isozaki, 'Ruins', in *Ryuji Miyamoto, Architectural Apocalypse*, Tokyo, 1988

26 reproduced in *Architectural Review*, January 1937

27 Sophie Ristelhueber, Beirut, London, 1984

28 August Sander's images of prewar Cologne are reproduced in Rolf Sachsse ed., *August Sander, Köln wie es war*, Cologne, 1988; ironically the bombing of the city in 1944 destroyed Sander's studio and many of his negatives.

29 R.H. Fuchs, 'The Eye Framed and Unframed', in *Jan Dibbets*,Walker Art Center, Minneapolis, 1987

30 commissioned by Actualites, London

31 Donald Bates, in *AA Files 19*, London, 1990

32 Gabriela Seifert and Gotz Stockmann, in the group *Formalhaut*.

PLATES

1 Bisson Frères, *Rheims Cathedral, West Front Portals, c. 1855-60*

Temple de Jupiter (Baalbek)

2 Tancrède Dumas, *Temple of Jupiter, Baalbek, 1880s*

3 P. H. Delamotte, Entrance to the Byzantine Court, Crystal Palace, 1850s

14

4 Eugène Atget, *The Corner of Rue Valette and The Pantheon, Paris, 1925*

5 Alfred Steiglitz, *Old New York, New New York, 1910*

6 Eduard Steichen, *The Flatiron Building, 1906*

7 A.L. Coburn, Broadway, New York, 1909/10

8 A.L. Coburn, *Singer Building, New York, 1909/10*

9 E.O. Hoppé, *Manhattan seen through the girders of Brooklyn Bridge, New York, 1919*

10 Sherill V. Schell, *Brooklyn Bridge, New York*, 1930s

11 Alexander Rodchenko, *Mosselprom House, Moscow, 1926*

12 Walker Evans, *Brooklyn Bridge, New York, 1929*

13 Florence Henri, *Wall through Window, 1930*

14 Erich Consemüller, *The Building as Stage (New Bauhaus Building)*, c.1927

15 Lucia Moholy, *Moholy-Nagy Dining-room*, 1926

16 Lucia Moholy, *View from Vestibule Window to Laboratory Block*, 1925/6

17 László Moholy-Nagy, *Berlin Radio Tower*, 1925

8 Herbert Bayer, *Transporter Bridge, Marseille,1928*

19 Herbert Bayer, *View from the Transporter Bridge, Marseille, 1928*

20 Werner Mantz, *Kölnische Zeitung, 1928*

21 Albert Renger-Patzsch, *Lubecker Blast Furnace, Winderhitzer, 1927*

22 Albert Renger-Patzsch, *Industrial Landscape, 1929*

23 Margaret Bourke-White, *Rosenbaum Grain Corporation, 1931*

24 Charles Sheeler, *Industry, 1932*

25 Karl-Hugo Schmölz, *Hotel Disch AG, Cologne, 1929*

26 John Heartfield, *The Choir of the Arms Industry, 1934*

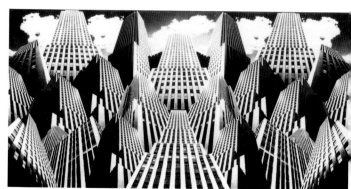

27 Thurman Rotan, *Untitled, c.1932*

28 Paul Citroen, *Metropolis*, 1923

29 Jim Dow, *Busch Stadium, St Louis, Missouri, 1982*

30 Joel Meyerowitz, *St Louis Arch, 1980*

31 Olivo Barbieri, *Hong Kong, Happy Valley, 1989*

32 Barbara Kasten, *Architectural Site 16, Whitney Museum of Art, 1987*

33 Georges Rousse, *Untitled, Marseille, 1986*

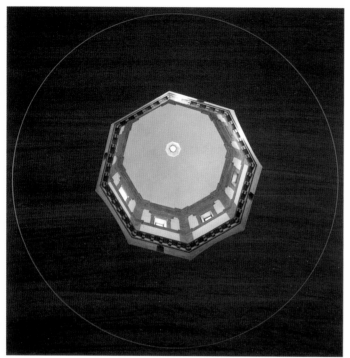 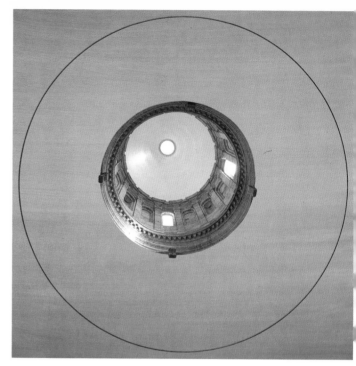

34 Jan Dibbets, *Three Cupolas, 1989-90*

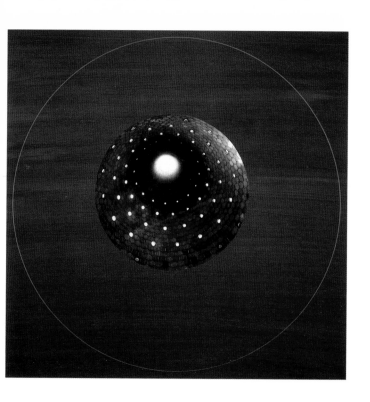

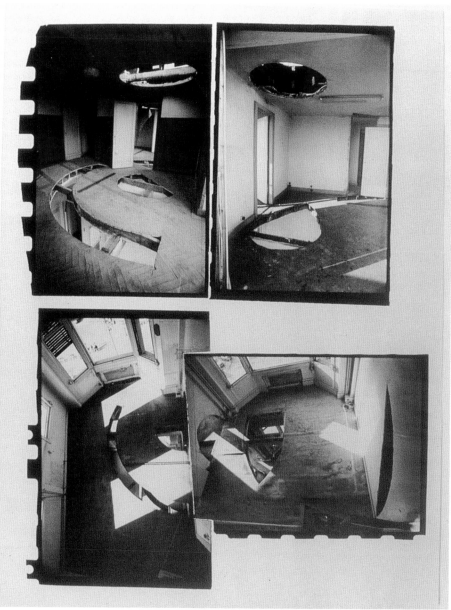

35 Gordon Matta-Clark, *Office Baroque*, 1977

36 Ezra Stoller, *Marine Midland Building, New York, 1967*

37 Richard Bryant, *Lloyds Building, London, 1986*

38 Otto Steinert, *Rheinstahl towerblock, Essen, 1961*

39 Bill Brandt, *Rainswept Roofs, 1930s*

40 Erich Angenendt, *Half-timbering, 1952*

41 Walker Evans, *Richard Perkins' Storefront, Moundville, Alabama, 1936*

42 Lewis Baltz, *West Wall, Unoccupied Industrial Structure, 20 Airway Drive, Costa Mesa,* from *The New Industrial Parks Near Irvine, California,* 1974

43 Lewis Baltz, *Construction detail, East Wall Xerox, 1821 Dyer Road, Santa Ana,* from *The New Industrial Parks Near Irvine, California,* 1974

44 Harry Callahan, *Skyscraper, Chicago, 1953*

45 Bob Thall, *Chicago, 1980*

46 Gabriele Basilico, *Dunkerque Harbour, 1984*

47 Gabriele Basilico, *Dunkerque Harbour, 1984*

45

48 Gabriele Basilico, *Dunkerque Harbour, 1984*

49 Gabriele Basilico, *Dunkerque Harbour, 1984*

50 Lewis Hine, *Man on a Mast, Empire State Building, New York, 1931*

1 Berenice Abbott, *Rockefeller Center, New York, 1930s*

52 John Davies, Steel VI, *Phase 11, Broadgate, 8 February 1989*

3 Catherine Wagner, *Arch Construction III, George Moscone Site, San Francisco, 1981*

54 Catherine Wagner, *View from the Wonderwall, Louisiana World Exposition, New Orleans, 1984*

Ryuji Miyamoto, *Asakusa Shochiku Movie Theatre by Seitaro Sengoku, Tokyo, 1984*

56 Axel Hütte, *London 1982-84*

57 Axel Hütte, *London 1982-84*

58 Bernd and Hilla Becher, *Gas Holder, Power Station, Essen Karnap, c.1970*

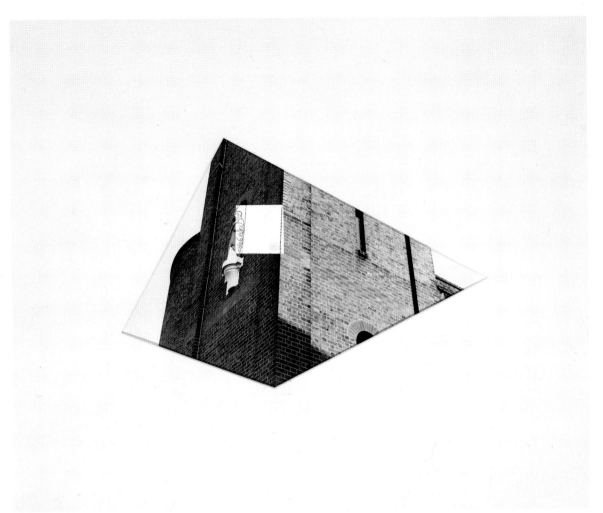

59 Julia Wood, *White Square, 1988*

60 Hélène Binet, *The House Without Walls by Daniel Libeskind, Milan Triennale, 1986*

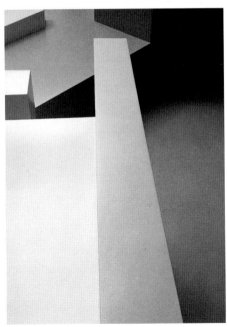

61 Judith Turner, *Peter Eisenman House, Thom Loft, New York, 1989*

62 Ottmar Hörl, *Die Grosse Vertikale II*, 1983

MORALITY, DARKNESS AND LIGHT: THE METROPOLIS IN PIC

Modern, or at least brand new, building entered photography in 1903 in the shape of the Flatiron Building, 'the latest thing in sky-scrapers', designed by Daniel H. Burnham for Winfield A. Stratton (a). A wedge-shaped building of twenty storeys situated at the point where Broadway intersects with 5th Avenue, it was

a Anon, *The Flatiron nearing completion, from* America at Work, *1903*

celebrated from the moment the scaffolding came down: '...the most wonderful building I guess there is on this earth, sir.' A contemporary source, John Foster Fraser writing in *America at Work* (1903), went into detail on its impact: 'The illustrated papers give two-page illustrations of it ...and an enterprising stationer has produced a three-folded photograph picture postcard of it ...It is the first thing a New Yorker takes you to see'.

b Alfred Stieglitz, *The Flatiron Building, 1903*

Foster remarked on its beauty, 'slender' and 'aquiline', but admired it as 'the latest fad in steel skeleton buildings' before pressing on to Pittsburgh's steelworks and hog killing and packing in Chicago.[1]

The Flatiron photographer of 1903 was Alfred Stieglitz, editor of his recently established *Camera Work*.[2] In his gravure (b) Stieglitz re-phrases the topical, steel-framed building in symbolist terms, as an essence, tidy and ethereal against a white winter sky. Parallel to the building he interjects a forked tree-trunk, which as it serves as an organic foil to the clean lines of the tower also repeats its

arrowhead ground-plan. It is a trope which attracts attention, at the expense both of the city's major talking point and of symbolism's impersonality. The object and the form, that is, are both overpowered by his, Stieglitz's, remark. His predilection was for the moment intensely apprehended: the moment as figured in the emergence of a trope, in a glance or gesture, or in the movement of light in vapour. In his later pictures of high-rise New York, c. 1930-31, taken from his gallery 'An American Place' (no. 509 Madison Avenue, 17th floor), the city functions as a sundial, register of the moment transmuting. Eduard Steichen's three-colour halftone of the Flatiron (plate 5), published in *Camera Work* in April 1906, represents time on hold, waiting with a cab-

c Berenice Abbott, *The Flatiron Building, 1938*

man. In 1939 a dingier, daylight version of the building rises opposite a Greyhound bus terminal in Berenice Abbott's *Changing New York* (c).[3] In 1906 the seated cab-man, twiggy branches, evening lights and the grey on grey of fog elaborate an extended moment; on May 18th 1938, when Abbott took her picture, time is nowhere on show, although, writ large and clear on a wall beyond, Sherwin-Williams Paints promise 'beauty and protection', under a claim to 'cover the earth'.

Between the winter of 1902-3 and that spring day in 1938 a history had unfolded in which the Flatiron had grown grimier as the noise of the world had grown louder, and more acceptable too. Photography's catholicity had increased, vis-à-vis architecture especially. Once upon a time it had been all pyramids and cathedrals, but by the time Abbott came to survey New York the predilection was for carpenter gothic, filling stations and hen houses. Architecture, though, had never lost its standing: it provided the idea around which much of the rest revolved. After all, for Stieglitz and for Steichen the Flatiron served as a foil, as a stable figure against which time-as-moment might be expressed. As an idea it could also be more

oppressive than sustaining, as the outlandish geometries of Paul Strand's *Wall Street* implied in October 1916, toward the end of the short history of *Camera Work*. Nevertheless, somewhere there existed, in imagination or in fact, an exemplary architecture; and in the 1920s that somewhere was located by the Great Lakes of the U.S. and Canada where towering white grain elevators and stores pointed the way towards a new architecture of primary forms (plate 23): in Le Corbusier's *Vers Une Architecture* of 1923 photographs of nine of these constitute 'Mass', his first of 'Three Reminders To Architects'(d); and then in 1926 in the stately gravures of Erich Mendelsohn's *Amerika*, Buffalo's silos make a giant mark.[4]

If *Vers Une Architecture*, with its range of aphorisms, exclamations and denunciations, is a riot, Ozenfant's *Foundations of Modern Art* (1928, with an English edition in 1931) is a

e Erich Mendelsohn, *The Schoken Stores by Night, Chemnitz, 1928-9, from Ozenfant,* Foundations of Modern Art, *1931, p.148*

scandal, compounded of 'wisdom', anecdotes and mischief, fancifully illustrated by photographs of, for example, Sir Austen Chamberlain in a monocle and top hat. Photography's tone in the 1920s was disrespectful to subversive; the subject of Werner Gräff's *Es Kommt der Neue Fotograf!* of 1929 knew neither gravity nor hierarchy. Among Ozenfant's cabaret turns, however, there are composed moments, one of which is provided by architecture in the form of Mendelsohn's 'Schocken Store in Chemnitz'(e), framed as an arc of a circle, part of a lit and ordered primary form – in contrast to its setting of *faits divers*. And there were texts too: in particular Paul Valéry's dramatised tract, *Eupalinos, or the architect*, in which a disembodied Socrates and others discussed the primacy of architecture and music; architecture, at the highest level, formed 'a sort of complete greatness within which we live', and it was valued in relation to an impurity in the other arts, where visible objects 'do not cease to be what they are, nor to mix their nature and their own significance with the design of him who uses them to express what he wishes'. In addition to the highest (temple) grade of architecture, Valéry identified a lower talkative grade of building, and one below that which was mute, and scorned. Eupalinos, the Greek master architect, worked under the tutelage of a body subject to an external nature of stones and trees in which right order

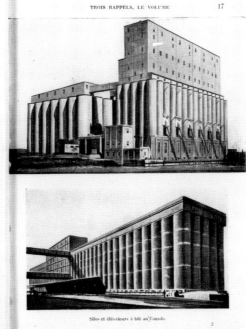

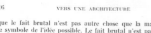

d Le Corbusier, *double-page spread from* Vers une Architecture, *1923*

f Lönberg-Holm, *from Erich Mendelsohn,* Amerika, *1928, p.76*

inhered – and Stieglitz, waiting and watching for the moment in which phenomena cohered, was an avatar. This art of equilibrium and true proportions depended on tranquillity and trust in relation to a primal world of waters, sand and clouds, but in the meantime the lower, talkative grades were on the march, and promising to 'cover the earth' with paint, print and neon.[5]

Despite Stieglitz and his ambitions for the medium, photography remained promiscuous. From the beginning it had been open to contingency, ready to show the pyramids, for example, as heaps of weathered stones, and battlefields as cart-tracks. And in the 1920s, as ever, it was receptive to any editor, anthologist or polemicist. At home with whatever was unresolved, it was especially at home in those negotiations between objectivity and order which characterised the 1920s. Some of that process is on show in Eric Mendelsohn's *Amerika,* one of photography's most awesome exhibits: a collection of 100 gravures, copyrighted in 1926, and reprinted thereafter – a 6th impression in 1928. Mendelsohn had designed the Einstein Tower at Potsdam (1921-2), a sculptural hybrid of a sand dune and a conning tower, and then, following visits to New York, Buffalo, Detroit and Chicago, put together *Amerika,* from his own photographs along with sixteen by the architects Lönberg-Holm of Detroit, and twenty-two by Karweik, his own chief architect. Mendelsohn's biases are obvious: one beautiful night picture of New York's streets (p.76, and by Lönberg-Holm, f) he approves as a 'Lichtzirkus .... im Rhythmus der Architektur' and all too rare. Evidently he moralises the New World in readily available terms: a shining city rises above informal, shadowy streets in which robotic individuals wander deserted and diminished; and one picture (p. 134) of such a solitary citizen on a park bench by an isolated sapling at the entry to Broadway makes his meaning clear; moreover, a notice reads 'danger', while on the sidelines Mendelsohn, like a impresario of apocalypse, intones: 'Baum und Ruhebank. Letzter Atem der letzten

Natur. Kaum gewagt, kümmerlich gegen die Härte der Steintürme' ('A tree and a bench. A last breath of a vanishing Nature. Hardly daring, feeble against the hardness of stone towers.'). That roughly is the story: a mutually determining relationship between an abbreviated citizenry, anonymous in trilbys and overcoats on the shaded pavements, and an enhanced, ethereal architecture, with the author introducing, explaining and lamenting.

Within the normality of *Amerika* lies a paradox, for Heaven has given rise to Hell: Mendelsohn's declared sympathies are all with humanity belittled on the sidewalks, but the book is just as clearly printed and arranged to do honour to that disproportionate city in the sky. *Amerika* puts on show a quandary, an ambivalence *vis-à-vis* the deplorable but alluring city. And the ambivalence spreads: not only is there something metaphysical and transcendental embodied in those stony towers, but at street level too there are irresistible invitations to linger in bad reality. Mendelsohn's connoisseurs of that reality were Lönberg-Holm, well represented in 'Das Groteske', the fifth of *Amerika's* six acts. The grotesque at issue was mainly advertisers' work: eg and especially, a thoroughfare on the outskirts of Detroit where the 'Moody Church of Pastor P.W. Philpott' speaks up between ads for Wrigley's chewing gum and Blue Valley Butter, 'Good – that's why millions use it' (although misidentified by Mendelsohn as Blue Band Margarine). By night and in neon bad reality was 'full of fantastic beauty', although by day that magic dissipated to disclose a huge hugger-mugger of trade and politics. The site for that morality was Broadway, by night and then by day (pp.130-132). Mendelsohn's objections involved a concern for cultural and categorical miscegenation, and indifference to hierarchy: chewing gum, margarine and religion, all equally billed with Grennan's Cakes, 'Every bite a delight'.

Two remarks suggest themselves apropos of *Amerika.* Firstly, there is the question of Mendelsohn's tone which is sometimes that of an impresario prepared to act as lyric poet and preacher. Between its sonorous

g László Moholy-Nagy, *Dessau Building Balconies, 1927*

commentaries and bold titles, *Amerika* sounds impressive: 'Das Weltzentrum – Das Geldzentrum', 'Das Gigantische', 'Das Groteske' – headings to sections 3,4 and 5 respectively. The truths of the 1920s, as of modernism in general, were negotiated less in the stillness of laboratories and studies than in public, in cafés, cabarets, theatres, editorial offices and in the streets. Even Valéry's decorous *Eupalinos* unfolds in what might be an Elysian spa café. In this *fortissimo* context photographs are adduced in support of the voice: *Amerika's* gravures are congruent with Mendelsohn's apocalyptic tone, just as Le Corbusier's vivid and surprising motifs, in *Vers Une Architecture* (1923) and *Urbanisme* (1924), brilliantly played, keep pace with his breathless patter.

If Mendelsohn was a strong poet and tragedian, and Le Corbusier a polemicist in a hurry, Moholy-Nagy and his colleagues at the Bauhaus were didacts with just as many points to make *and to illustrate.* Thus photography was carried out with illustration in mind, with an eye to, for example, analyses and expositions of space, movement, material (L. Moholy-Nagy's table of contents in *the new vision* c.1929). Under the terms of this rubric the most useful photographs were the most circumscribed: diagonals, or grids, or lights, or patterns, etc (g). Anything ambiguous could only interrupt the spiel.[6] Voices, instructing and itemising, took precedence in relation to pictures which excluded the kind of aberrant, random encounters to be met with at ground level; Bauhaus photography, in particular, looks upward and outward away from the confusion and debris of streets and battlefields (away from the telluric art and reportage of the Great War). If such photographers as László Moholy-Nagy, Lucia Moholy and Werner Mantz meant to express an idealising world of light framed and tabulated, they intended at the same time something like a stage on which humanity might act to advantage, gesturing and declaiming, as on the dustjacket of the Bauhaus catalogue of 1938 (Museum of Modern Art, New York). Bauhaus building, characterised by balconies, podia and rostrums, catered for histrionics of the kind enacted by the *Treppenwitz* group for Erich Consemüller, T. Lux Feininger and Herbert Bayer in 1927 (plate 14). At the same time the emphatic and unimpeded orthogonals of the new architecture, as staged and interpreted in the new photography, spelled out destiny as a good calculable infinity, of the kind charted across the reticulated surface of the Bauhaus laboratory block (plate 16).

Secondly, there is more to be gathered from *Amerika's* ambivalence. Mendelsohn's topic, the metropolis in relation to its residents and victims, had been an avant-garde priority since futurism. In the many vanguard theatrical projects of futurists, Dadaists and constructivists, where metropolitan futures were envisioned and enacted, extremes predominate: futurists identified with the machine assassin; Dada put the metropolitan sickness on show, said 'yes' to alienation; or mankind was assimilated into a reformed order of machines, or the metropolitan milieu was projected as an enlivened 'montage of attractions' (Eisenstein)[7] as in Paul Citroen's *Metropolis* of 1923 (plate 28). *Amerika* may end with a resolved, futuristic final act, 'Das Neue – Das Kommende', but its mood is too doubtful to qualify it as a work of the early 1920s. It looks forward, rather, to the writing of the objectivists, to the city (Berlin) as represented by Joseph Roth in *Flight without End* (1927) and by Erich Kästner in *Fabian: The Story of a Moralist* (1931).[8] Roth (dateline Paris) completed his foreword thus: 'I have invented nothing, made up nothing. The question of "poetic invention" is no longer relevant. Observed fact is all that counts'. Yet filtering through Roth's inventories of street life come murmurings of carnival and of marvels, quickly reined in, neutralised (and intensified) by talk of frankfurters and of shoe-laces. Fabian, another powerless random traveller in the style of Roth's Tunda, recognises a similar potential in objects, but a potential no sooner suspected than denied: eg at Uncle Pell's Amusement Park, three streets from Berlin's Weddingplatz, he comes across a lucky wheel dispensing lump sugar, butter and bacon, lingeringly itemised to keep at bay, and in being, the temptation to speak of a wheel of fortune. Fabian drowned in an incident, and Tunda found himself, aged thirty-two, superfluous on the Place de la Madeleine, on 27th August 1926, at four in the afternoon. The writers tell of strain and disappointments intensified by nostalgia for a future which had been promised. The drama of the 1920s – Amerika – Berlin – Place de la Madeleine – involved absolutes: once-and-for-all answers to the problem of life in the metropolis, ostentatious and abject capitulations to the pell-mell, in addition to crippling doubts.

The arts of the 1920s were frontline arts adapted to meet the tactical requirements of the moment. You manoeuvred or went under; Walter Benjamin, in his famous *Small History of Photography* (1931), concluded that Sander's pictures in *Das Antlitz der Zeit* (1930) amounted to a training manual for the wary citizens of tomorrow; and Eugène Atget's newly printed pictures of Paris (plate 4) were admired for their political possibilities: they gave 'free play to the politically educated eye'.[9] Benjamin placed Atget with the avant-garde of the 1920s, with the photographs of details: 'here a piece of balustrade, there a tree-top whose bare branches crisscross a gas lamp, or a gable wall, or a lamp-post with life-buoy bearing the name of a town'. But by 1930, in Paris at least, the agenda seems to have changed to include priorities unrecognised by Benjamin. It seems that for some time the Parisian sub-culture from which photographs emerged had been more interested in worlds apart, and the more secretive the better. Roth's *Flight Without End* ends with a list of Parisian engrossments, which might have been taken as a work-sheet by the post-New Photographers: 'beggars deloused themselves on the banks of the Seine, loving couples embraced in the Bois de Boulogne, children played on the roundabouts in the public gardens'.

Benjamin's vanguard list of pieces of balustrade and lamp-posts is unpeopled;

h Germaine Krull, *Cabane de Zoniers*, from Andre Warnod, Visages de Paris, 1930, p. 275

Roth's panorama of Paris, on the other hand, 'objective' or not, is loud with talk, work and traffic. There are distinct old world elements in the newer reportage, along with signs of indifference to the Modern: eg André Warnod's *Visages de Paris* (1930) depends on photographs by Germaine Krull, a photographer praised by Benjamin, and a specialist, earlier in the 1920s in dramatic industrial diagonals (published in *Métal*, 1927); in a concluding chapter, 'Charmes de Paris', 1930, Krull shows a spectacular and busy city, but cleansed of evil and gaiety, in contrast to the earlier 'L'Avant Guerre' anachronistically composed of picturesque marginals (*zoniers*) and delousing clochards (h). Modernity, in terms of Krull's modernistically searchlit city of 1930, was impersonal and limitless; the prewar era, even if also put together from contemporary ingredients, was an intimate composite: carnival, café, small hotels, narrow streets, market stalls and close, challenging encounters. Where the brusque industrial fragments of the 1920s spoke, as fragments, of the social totality at issue, the new reportage dealt in imponderables of the kind imposed by chance and intrusive encounters with the other *in extremis*: drunkard, clochard, zonier, gypsy mother (from among Krull's Parisian cast).[10] The subject of this new economy of images, of whatever sort, was the self in perplexity, at a loss for the kind of articulate response dictated in the modernist heyday.

Where the old modernism was premised on a hierarchy of respectworthy themes, the new archaism presumed only encounters and a protean subject stimulated to unpredictable flights of fancy by the idea of secrecy and exclusion. But what was only a tendency in Krull's anachronistic 'L'Avant Guerre' of 1930 was soon consolidated: by 1933 Brassaï's treatment of secrecy in *Paris de Nuit* was emphatic. The tendency explored by Krull drew on a myth of Paris as constituted of secret, and intriguing 'worlds' ; its epic was Emile Chautard's *La Vie Etrange de l'Argot* of 1931, 700 pages of the language of prostitutes, pimps and prisoners, and rich in coinages of *l'avant guerre*. In photography the tendency was forwarded most of all by the publication (by Henri Jonquières in Paris and Leipzig) of 96 gravures by Eugène Atget (d.4.8.1927). 'Atget's' intentions were signalled in the opening image of the book of 1930. The image is of nothing more than a darkened

doorway and a window, on the sill of which stand two window boxes, with a crossboard which supports a pot plant: evidence of the habits and character of the concierge, indicated by an inscription and arrow. Concierge was a term synonymous with talk, secrets, confessions. Here is Céline reflecting on the meaning of the word, c. 1930, in his *Journey to the End of the Night*, and apropos of Lola in New York: 'But there wasn't a concierge in her house. There wasn't a concierge in the whole of New York. A city devoid of concierges can't have any life, any atmosphere, it's as dull as soup without salt or pepper, a wretched thin brew. Oh, those choice morsels! Titbits gathered in boudoirs, kitchens and attics, dripping, cascading downstairs to the concierge, who sits there in the midst of life – what a rich infernal harvest! Some of our concierges at home succumb at their posts; laconic, coughing, adorable, bewildered, they're consumed and stupefied by so much Truth, like martyrs to it.'[11]

Atget – Lichtbilder/Atget – Photographe de Paris looks like a collection of metaphors which might stand for aspects of the city in general: trade, transport, the underworld; but what sort of categories exactly must remain forever doubtful; and at the same time details promise to tell a story: eg it has been raining, which might explain disorder among a clutch of deserted handcarts. Interpretation, which involves a sifting and entertainment of memories and terms, is as unavoidable as interminable. Speculation is only increased by an iconography of doors, windows and facades: provocative signs of exclusion from interiors where the truth is probably only known to such as Céline's concierges.

Atget's haunted doorways and suggestive urban residua were troublesome in their turn. If the bespoke industrial fragments favoured by the post-war modernists defined their clients' interests too narrowly, Atget's dream avenues, by contrast, had any and every destination imaginable. Benjamin, for instance, conjured the idea of a good, purposeful Atget in opposition to a hypothetical photography of aura – which could almost have been based on the fogged gravures of *Atget – Lichtbilder*. Berenice Abbott, saviour of the Atget archive, applied 'Atget' to New York; among the 97 pictures in *Changing New York* (1939) there are small-scale annotated facades in the Parisian manner, and studies of street peddlers lately (1938) banned and 'corralled into modern enclosed markets, municipally operated'. Abbott's writer, Elizabeth McCausland, names and lists in time to the pictures, and her sympathies lie with the suppressed peddlers and store owners. The virtue of the cheaper stores, restaurants, news-stands and barber shops was that they allowed reading and enumeration: 20c for an Electric Massage, 10c for Pigs Feet and Kraut – and more, by the Blossom Restaurant, 103 Bowery. Despite affinities with Old Paris, Abbott's, and McCausland's, New York differs from the precursor city chiefly in terms of insistent moral and practical guidance.

The modernism of the 1920s had been premised on selflessness, transcending local and even national affiliations; and the *zonier* myth of 1930 (Krull, Atget, Brassaï) was romantic at heart. Modernist idioms, however, were increasingly associated, towards the end of the 1920s, with the polemics surrounding Russia's Five Year Plan, undertaken in 1927; and the *zonier* aesthetic was one of shadows and dreams: eg Krull's *Marseille* of 1935 keeps company with a poetic text, by André Suares, which tells the stained city as an odyssey or Mediterranean melodrama. Krull's *Marseille* was a last enchanted report from the underworld, and even here there is plenty of evidence of daylit labour.

If modernism's turn was best served by structures which put line and mass on show to dramatic effect, and if the classic place of the *zonier* artists was a *maison close*, or some other house of secrets, the new documentary photography of the later 1930s opted for more legible sites which allowed for decipherment, and for the kind of enactment entailed by decipherment: the surfaces of *Changing New York*, for example, are alive with scripts which recount daily life in detail. In Walker Evans's *American Photographs* (September 1938) decipherment is of the essence, less in the celebrated Part One of 50 images which unwinds as a cryptic narrative through youth and age, country and town, than in a usually overlooked Part Two of 37 architectural images. The onus in Abbott's metropolis is literally on reading, on the city as a text; Evans's small towns (i), by contrast invite gauging and assessment of lines and relationships in the style of a carpenter or surveyor; for almost every structure on show is constituted of a fascia inscribed by shadow cast by columns, awnings, screens, grills and grids. Just as darkness was the ambience proper to the dreamworld photography of 1930 (sustained anachronistically into the late 1930s in Britain by Bill Brandt), daylight was that of the documentarists for whom the light of day was a prerequisite to understanding.

i Walker Evans, *Ossining, New York, 1930*

Footnotes

1 All citations from John Foster Fraser's first chapter, *The Newest New York*.

2 The whole of *Camera Work* is illustrated in *Camera Work: A Pictorial Guide*, edited by Marianne Margolis for Dover Publications, New York, 1978.
Many of Stieglitz's later architectural pictures appear in *America and Alfred Stieglitz*, edited by Waldo Frank, etc., for the Literary Guild, New York, 1934.

3 Berenice Abbott's *Changing New York* of 1939 was republished as *New York in the Thirties* by Dover Publications, New York, 1973.

4 Le Corbusier's *Vers une Architecture* was translated into English in 1927 by Frederick Etchells and published by The Architectural Press, London; a facsimile of that edition is frequently reprinted by Holt, Rinehart and Winston.
In 1929 Etchells also translated the frequently republished *Urbanisme* of Le Corbusier (1924): *The City of Tomorrow and its Planning*.

5 Paul Valéry, *Eupalinos, or the architect*, translated with a preface by William M. Stewart, London, 1932; for Eupalinos's credit *credo* see pp. 24-33.

6 *the new vision: Fundamentals of design painting sculpture architecture* was also No. 1 in the series *The New Bauhaus Books*, London, 1939.

7 For the metropolis as a topic in avant-garde theatre see the essay *The Stage as "Virtual City": From Fuchs to the Totaltheater* in Manfredo Tafuri's *The Sphere and the Labyrinth*, published in paperback by the MIT Press, London, 1990.

8 Joseph Roth's *Die Flucht ohne Ende* was translated by David le Vay and published as an Everyman Classic, London, 1984. Kästner's *Fabian*, translated by Cyrus Brooks, was published by Cape, London, 1932, and again (without omissions) by Libris, London, 1990.

9 Walter Benjamin's *A Small History of Photography* appears in the collection of essays *One-Way Street*, edited by Susan Sontag and translated by E. Jephcott and K. Shorter for New Left Books, London, 1979, pp.240-257.

10 Many of Germaine Krull's photographs are published in *Germaine Krull: Fotografien, 1922-1966*, Rheinishches Landesmuseum, Bonn, 1977, including nothing from her Parisian and Marseille reportages.

11 Louis-Ferdinand Céline's *Voyage au Bout de la Nuit* (1932) was translated by John Marks and published, with a wrapper photograph by André Kertész, by Chatto & Windus, London, 1934 (concierge details, p.223).

THE SPECIALIST EYE ROBERT ELWALL

In 1979, the teacher and photographer Tom Picton launched a withering attack on the contemporary architectural photograph, which he dismissed as 'the craven image', a lifeless piece of flattering deception foisted on an unsuspecting public by an unholy alliance of architect, photographer and art editor.[1] Picton's assertion that architectural photography had degenerated into a form of advertising, and the fierce debate it provoked, served to highlight the fact that photographs had become the indispensable currency of architectural exchange, and underlined important developments since the turn of the century in the way photographs were perceived and used, and in the relationship between photographer and architect, as well as between architect and the public.

While architects such as George Devey and John Loughborough Pearson assembled impressive collections of photographs as aids to their own designs, while historians like James Fergusson used photographs to construct a new kind of comparative architectural history, and while the images of the architectural photographers, Bedford Lemere and Co., were disseminated in large numbers, throughout the 19th century the photograph's role as a means of architectural documentation was limited by its incompatibility with the printing press. Only with the advent of the half-tone block in the 1880s and its general application during the following decade did it finally became possible to print photographs and type together in a single operation. As a result, a new crop of architectural magazines dedicated to the use of this new technology, most notably *Architectural Review* (1896) and *Country Life* (1897), sprang into existence. Henceforth architectural magazines such as these were to be in the forefront of developments in British architectural photography, employing the leading exponents, giving them access to a large new audience, and ensuring that their

work would in future be most commonly seen not in its original form but in reproduction. In turn photography assumed an increasingly important role in the design, presentation and appeal of these magazines.

This radical transformation in the way photographs reached their audience occasioned no sudden changes in the way buildings were photographed. Although the pictorialist approach of Frederick Evans influenced a generation of amateur photographers, his striking explorations of light and space had no lasting effect on mainstream architectural photography. They served merely to emphasise the widening rift between amateurs and professionals which was especially evident in architectural image-making. The evocative country house views of Charles Latham notwithstanding, the journals were full of worthy, but unremarkable record photographs by photographers such as Edwin Dockree and the long-lasting Bedford Lemere, using small stops and long exposures to concentrate on the sharp definition of overall forms. The pictures were usually taken in dull, diffused light, avoiding dramatic effects of light and shade in order to preserve vital detail. The camera was placed to obtain not expressive effect, but maximum information on each plate. T. H. B. Scott, architect and Fellow of the Royal Photographic Society, lamented in 1923, 'Architectural photography is at a very low ebb ... We yearn for good photographic appreciation of modern architectural expression.'[2]

As Scott wrote, a new vision, which paid increased attention to the man-made rather than the natural world and which thus helped to revitalise architectural photography, was taking shape in Europe and the United States. The new post-war order was to be created by industry, revealed in a machine-inspired architecture and evangelised by the photographer. Images of contemporary architecture and engineering, such as the

coldly analytical studies of New Objectivity photographers like Werner Mantz, were presented as icons of this new utopian sensibility. At the same time the introduction of more versatile cameras, especially the Leica in 1924, encouraged experimentation with different points of view. Close-ups, worm's- and bird's-eye views characterised the so-called New Photography, revealing novel and more dynamic possibilities for photographing buildings.

The New Photography's fascination with geometry and abstraction, and its emphasis on the sublime were inimical to the British photographic tradition which revelled in the small-scale and the picturesque. The hostile reception it received and the lull in building activity after the War meant that British architectural photographers were slow to assimilate its ideas. Such reserve is seen in

a Frank Yerbury, *Neuerburg Cigarette Factory, Hamburg, 1926*

work of F R Yerbury (plate 63;a), Secretary
the Architectural Association, and, for a
ort time, official photographer to the
chitectural Review . Yerbury's overriding
ncern was to record the exciting
chitectural developments that were taking
ace abroad and his arresting photographs
ublished in Architect & Building News to
company a series of over 150 articles by
ward Robertson) exercised a profound
luence on a whole generation of British
chitects by giving them their first
quaintance with international modernism.
st as he found it impossible, however, to
cept the harsher, more full-blown
anifestation of modernism in architecture
referring instead the softer forms of Dutch
German brick architecture, or the Swedes'
nsitive use of traditional materials) so only
casionally do we catch fleeting glimpses of

the New Photography in Yerbury's work,
notably in his swan-song *One Hundred
Photographs* (1935). Though radical in his
choice of subject, comparison of his treatment
of one of the key subjects of the New
Photography, the Transporter Bridge at
Marseille, with that of the Bauhaus
photographer, Herbert Bayer, underlines the
essential conservatism of Yerbury's technique.

The *Architectural Review*, which since its
inception had placed important emphasis on
the quality of its photographic illustrations,
became, in the more doctrinaire 1930s,
increasingly committed to the cause of
modern architecture, which as an essentially
alien import, required strenuous efforts to sell
it to a sceptical British public. The *Review*
deployed an arsenal of formidable weapons in
the battle – a rigorous selection of buildings
for inclusion, fervent articles by writers

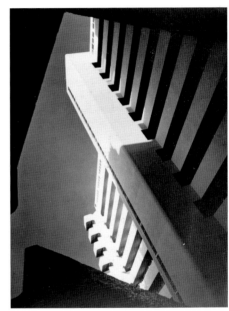

c Dell & Wainwright, *Embassy Court, Brighton, 1935*

dedicated to the cause, eye-catching page
layouts (b), innovative typography and, above
all, dazzling photographs supplied by its
official photographers from 1930 to 1946,
Mark Oliver Dell and H. L. Wainwright.

More than anyone else Dell and Wainwright
(plates 65,66;c) are responsible for our
enduring image of Thirties architecture: flat-
roofed, horizontal-windowed, box-shaped
houses which (thanks in part to the
photographers' use of coloured filters) stand
white and immaculate against dramatic dark
skies. With strong shadows accentuating form
and line or providing relief to a smooth
expanse of wall, their glass-hard images leap
from the page with irresistibly seductive
power. Theirs was a photography of strident
contrast, angular geometry and austere
precision which utilised, albeit in a diluted form
and with an unwieldy Sanderson plate camera,
the tipped views and juxtaposition of elements
within the frame typical of the New

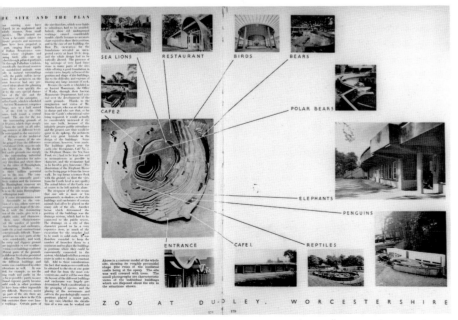

Double-page spread on Dudley Zoo, Architectural Review, *November 1937*

d Dell & Wainwright, *Ramsgate Municipal Airport*, 1937

Photography. Their photograph of the new Daily Express Building, Fleet Street (1931), shot from below to give emphasis to the black Vitriolite and glass cladding and to allow the inclusion of St Bride's, artfully suggests that this is a modernist structure fit to stand alongside Wren's church in the great tradition of British architecture – a continuity interrupted only by the kind of Victorian muddle to be glimpsed between the two. The photograph was more than an excitingly dynamic image – it was a strongly composed statement that modern architecture was on the right track. Similarly, their view of *Ramsgate Municipal Airport* (d), with the terminal building perfectly counterpointing the fuselage of the plane in the foreground, emphasises the machine aesthetic of the new architecture, as the American photographer Ken Hedrich was later to do in his photographs of Albert Kahn's Detroit car factories.

Although the photographer's task during the 1930s was rendered more exacting by the prevalence of indirect lighting, the trend away from the cluttered, dark Victorian interior towards lighter, more open rooms dependent for their effect on flush surfaces, simple and economic lines and frequent use of reflective materials such as mirror glass and chromium, afforded photographers like Dell and Wainwright new dramatic possibilities. Their use of expressive camera angles was combined with an unerring eye for the repetitive patterns to be found in modern architecture, whether it was the concrete fins of the Wembley swimming baths (1934) or a row of shower units at the *Pioneer Health Centre, Peckham* (1935) (plate 65).

Despite such images Dell and Wainwright had no real commitment to modernism. Dell, a lifelong friend of Alvin Langdon Coburn, had helped found the RPS Pictorial Group in 1921 and retired in 1946 to concentrate on landscape and nature subjects. The photographers usually worked under the close control of the editorial staff or the architects concerned – architectural photography had become too important a matter to be left to the photographer alone. Indeed, much of the persuasive force of Dell and Wainwright's images stems from the creative way in which

they were used by the *Review's* art editors who were influenced by German illustrated magazines of the 1920s, the work of the Design and Industries Association and, especially, by the French periodical, *Arts et Métiers*, which began publication in 1927. Selected photographs were spread over the whole page and often bled to the edge or beyond in specially folded sheets, and coloured printing inks and glossy paper enhanced the journal's appearance. Shorn of their white borders, photographs became fully integrated elements of the magazine, not illustrated appendages. Text and image were indissolubly linked and mutually reinforcing. Photomontage, composite pictures and suggestive juxtapositions of images were all used to satisfy the *Review's* guiding principle that every page should contain a surprise. The emphasis also shifted away from the individual image – one picture no longer had to tell the full story. Dell and Wainwright's photographs were designed to be read as an unfolding sequence – best shown in their series of the new Royal Institute of British Architects (1934), carefully choreographed to resemble a

e John Havinden, *Lawn Road Flats*, 1934

movie camera's exploration of the subject.

More whole-hearted in his commitment to modernism and the New Photography was John Havinden, who was one of the first to exploit the new opportunities afforded to photographers by the growing use of advertising by industrial and design companies. Although only occasionally concerned with architecture, he produced daring and innovative photographs that demonstrate an informed concern for structure and materials and the delineation of formal abstraction – witness his striking view of the *Lawn Road Flats, Hampstead* (1934;e) and, most memorably of all, his wonderfully expressive pictures of the *Penguin Pool, London Zoo* (1934), reproduced in the *Architectural Review*, which managed precisely to capture the sculptural quality of the pool's interlocking spiral ramps.

Another photographer whose work was sometimes featured in the *Review*, but more often in the *Architect & Building News*, was Leo Herbert Felton (plate 64;f), a friend of Dell and a fellow member of the RPS Pictorial Group. Sir John Summerson, who was assistant editor of the Architect & Building News at the time, recalls that Felton had 'an incorrigible preference for picturesque views over disciplined recording' [3] – hardly surprising for a friend and admirer of Frederick Evans. Felton's architectural photographs seem to hold the picturesque tendency in check and his work shows a consistently high standard of technical excellence, though unfortunately it was not

f Herbert Felton, *Olympia Interior Staircase*, 1930

always reproduced to best effect.

The 1930s was a decade of unprecedented vigour in British architectural photography. As the number of architectural journals steadily grew, competition intensified and helped raise photographic standards, as editors realised that the provision of good half-tone illustration could be crucial to their circulation figures. The photograph, as architect H. S. Goodhart-Rendel remarked, was 'not only illustration but news.' [4] The decade also witnessed a keen

lic interest in architecture and, as the
holic range of its subject matter testifies,
Architectural Review in particular looked to
ract a non-specialist audience for whom
otographs were more intelligible than
hitectural drawings. Contemporaries
reed that, for good or ill, the camera was
coming the normal medium through which
w buildings were presented – a state of
airs symbolised by the replacement in 1931
Academy Architecture, which reproduced
e drawings shown at the Royal Academy, by
chitecture Illustrated, a monthly full of fine
otographs, only the occasional plan, and no
xt apart from the captions. Confronted by
ch demand, the number of photographers
le to make a living mainly from architectural
otography increased. Sydney Newbery,
ewart Bale, John Maltby and Millar and
rris all produced high quality record images
this time.

f more photographs were used, they were
o used more purposefully. Whereas in the
th century architects complained that the
ailability of collections of random
otographs had contributed to the rampant
lecticism of the period by making 'all the art
the past the property of the present',5 in
34 the architect Sir Reginald Blomfield
umbled that photography was responsible
r advertising the Modern Movement as 'the
e and only gospel of artistic salvation'.6
milarly, once architects realised that the
otographers could choose to use their
meras not only to record, but to interpret,
tter or even deceive, and that their pictures
ere likely to be widely reproduced, they
anted to ensure that they were part of that
oice. Noting the way his mentor Sir Edwin
tyens's career had been nurtured by
equent features in Country Life, Oliver Hill
as but one of a number of architects who
refully orchestrated the way in which their
uildings were photographed. The photograph
ad thus become a tool of persuasion and
blicity.

In March 1937 Architectural Review and its
merican counterpart, Architectural Record,
wapped editorial control for the month. A
omparison of the photographs reproduced
uggests that Dell and Wainwright were more
onservative in their interpretation of modern
rchitecture than American photographers
uch as F.S. Lincoln, his country's leading pre-
Var professional. After the War Lincoln's
antle was assumed by the large firms of
edrich-Blessing in Chicago and Ezra Stoller
lates 69,70) in New York. Their images,

The richness of east end life is replaced by monotony and inhumanity

h Patrick Ward, *spread from 1st 'Manplan' issue, 'Frustration',* Architectural Review, *September 1969*

such as Hedrich's *Fallingwater* of 1937 (plate
67) or Stoller's *Seagram Building, New York*
(1958) (marketed through his powerful
distribution company Esto Photographics),
were endlessly reproduced and, together with
the Los Angeles-based Julius Shulman's
portraits of West Coast Case Study Houses
(plate 68), greatly influenced architects in
Britain and elsewhere and helped consolidate
the Modern Movement. Nevertheless, it was
Dell and Wainwright who established the norm
for British architectural photography after the
Second World War. Their style perhaps
reached its ultimate expression in the work of
Richard Einzig, characterised as it was by a
strong sense of formal composition with
buildings often shot head-on to resemble
architects' elevational drawings in a manner
reminiscent of the New Objectivity
photographers. Einzig's stern images and
preoccupation with flat planes are well shown
in his treatment of James Stirling's *History
Library, Cambridge* (g).

Almost from the beginning, however, this
style of photography was criticised for lacking
humanity and flattering buildings to a
pernicious degree. Michael Rothenstein argued
perceptively in 1946[7] that modern
architecture had become a colourless idiom
largely because of the ubiquity of black and
white images which were so forceful that
architects were in danger of developing 'the
photographic eye'. He attacked
photographers for photographing only in clear
sunlight when the relationship between
different volumes and contrasting planes was
shown to great advantage, and for ignoring
the realities of the grey British weather. 'The
modern architect,' Rothenstein concluded,
'imitates the photographer; he builds with
lights and shadows, with black and white'. The
result was 'an architecture deficient in
chromatic values.'

Such criticism fostered a photojournalistic
approach to architectural photography, an
attempt to show buildings in use and in their
setting. Ironically, this approach had its origins
in the articles on environmental damage or
neglected aspects of the architectural heritage

which *Architectural Review* published in the
inter-war years. These had been illustrated
with lively, informal snapshots taken with small
format cameras by the authors or the editorial
staff – John Piper's 'The Nautical Style' issue
of January 1938 is a typical example. In a
similar vein, the mid-1950s 'Outrage'(i) and
'Counter-Attack' issues, edited and part-
illustrated by Ian Nairn, used photographs in a
polemical fashion to campaign for
improvements in urban design. These
campaigns, by drawing attention to the
importance of the space between buildings
and the buildings' relationship to them,
encouraged photographers to pay increased
attention to context. The *Review*'s use of
photographs in such a manner culminated in
the eight 'Manplan' issues published between
September 1969 and September 1970 (h),
which assessed the state of the nation in
architecture and planning and found it wanting.
This time, however, the images were not
supplied by amateurs, but by specially
commissioned photojournalists such as Peter
Baistow, Tony Ray-Jones and Tim Street-
Porter. With the aid of 35mm cameras and the

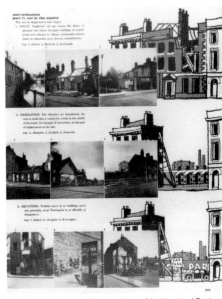

i Anti-Urbanism, *from 'Outrage' issue of* Architectural Review, *June 1955*

Richard Einzig, *Cambridge History Library, 1968*

Above: looking down into one of the courtyards
Below: the access deck, wide enough for milk trolleys, children's games, a true equivalent of the communal street

k John Donat, *Goffs Bloodstock Sales, County Kildare, 1975*

j Roger Mayne, *Park Hill, Sheffield,* page from Architectural *Design, September, 1961*

frequent use of claustrophobic wide-angle images, they portrayed a harsh reality, the alarming deterioration in the quality of people's everyday lives. Unused to having their work questioned in this way, many architects were outraged and cancelled their subscriptions. This was not the first time photojournalistic methods had been applied to architecture. In September 1961 Roger Mayne had contributed to *Architectural Design's* special issue on Sheffield (j), but here the photographs of the now notorious *Park Hill Estate,* were used to emphasise the benefits of a carefully planned development from the inhabitants' point of view. The difference in mood between these photographs and the 'Manplan' series neatly encapsulates the initial optimism of the 1960s and its subsequent disillusionment.

Significantly, none of the 'Manplan'

photographers were at the time dependent primarily on architectural photography for their livelihoods. The architectural photographer (though he dislikes the label) who most epitomises this photojournalistic approach, John Donat (plate 72;k), prefers to use miniature, hand-held cameras to capture 'an experience of a slice of time in the life of a building,'[8] even if this sometimes means sacrificing technical perfection to obtain a 'live' picture. Donat, who admires the work of Cartier-Bresson and acknowledges a debt to Roger Mayne and Tim Street-Porter, believes the context reveals the architecture, and accordingly portrays buildings in their environment and in use, The reportage method of Donat and others has, however, been undermined by the tremendous explosion in the use of colour photography since the 1970s caused by advances in offset reproduction and the demands of advertisers.

While the proliferation of colour images has arguably contributed significantly to the emergence of Post-Modernism – and partly countered Rothenstein's criticisms – it has also seen in photography a reversion to the idealised formal abstraction identified with Dell and Wainwright and further fuelled the debate inspired by Tom Picton about the responsibilities of the architectural photographer. When Picton wrote, architectural photography had become a specialist art reaching a specialist audience through specialist outlets, a means of

reassurance to a demoralised profession out of public favour. Photographer and architect were drawn into closer alliance than ever before. When the interwar photographers were members of professional *photographic* bodies the new breed who emerged after World War have largely come from *architectural* backgrounds – Sam Lambert, Richard Einzig (plate 71), John Donat, Richard Bryant (plates 37,74), for example, all received architectural training – reflecting a belief that architectural photography requires specialist knowledge. During the 19th century architects were content to allow architectural photographers to trade on the illusion that the camera was a mechanical recording device which produced 'the genuine presentment of the object under consideration';[9] since then they have come to recognise photography as a creative, interpretative act and, as a result, they naturally wish to have a say in how their buildings are photographed. As a professional the architectural photographer's first obligation must be to his client even if the resultant images outstrip reality. The photographer's continuing dilemma was well summed up in a witty, but poignant, aphorism uttered by Goodhart-Rendel back in 1938: 'The modern architectural drawing is interesting, the photograph is magnificent, the building is an unfortunate but necessary stage between the two'.[10]

Footnotes

1 See the *Architects' Journal,* July 25, 1979, p.175-190 and Aug.1, 1979, p.225-242

2 *Building News,* Dec.21, 1923, p.688-689

3 Letter from Sir John Summerson to the author, Jan.1988

4 *Architect & Building News,* Apr.9, 1937, p.33

5 T R Smith, 'The Practice of an Architect,' *British Quarterly,* 1880, p.426

6 Sir Reginald Blomfield, *Modernisms* (London: Macmillan, 1934), p.51

7 See 'Colour and Modern Architecture, or the Photographic Eye' in *Architectural Review,* June 1946, p.159-163

8 John Donat, *Architecture through the Lens* (London : Pidgeon Audio Visual [1980])

9 William and Mary Howitt, 'Preface', *Ruined Abbeys and Castles of Great Britain* (London : Bennett, 1982)

10 Quoted in 'Bliss Was It in That Dawn to Be Alive' : an Interview with John Brandon-Jones, *Architectural Design,* 1979, no.10/11, p.98

PLATES

63 Frank Yerbury, *Anti-God Museum in St Isaac's Cathedral, Leningrad, 1932*

Herbert Felton, *Dudley Penguin Pool, 1937*

66 Dell & Wainwright, *London Electricity Showroom, Regent Street, 1938*

Dell & Wainwright, *Pioneer Health Centre, Peckham, 1935*

67 Bill Hedrich, *Bear Run, Fallingwater*, 1937

68 Julius Shulman, *Living Area of Pierre Koenig's Case Study House No. 22*, 1960

Ezra Stoller, S.C. Johnson Administration Building and Research Tower, 1944

70 Ezra Stoller, *TWA Terminal, JFK Airport, New York, 1962*

Richard Einzig, *Pompidou Centre, 1978*

72 John Donat, *Dunelm House, Durham and Kingsgate Footbridge, 1966*

73 Tim Street-Porter, *Orange County, 1985*

Richard Bryant, *Vitra Museum, Weil, 1990*

AVAILABLE FOR VIEWING JANET ABRAMS

For what do we look at photographs of buildings? Or rather, let us step back a pace...but carefully, with our head tilted sideways over one shoulder, watching out for whatever snares lie on the ground behind. So, eye to the viewfinder, keeping the target still in sight, lest it scurries away or subtly transmutes while we're not looking: why do we take photographs of buildings? And why do we pore over them, published on the glossy pages of a million magazines?

I ask these questions because they are the dumb ones which, literally, never seem to get a hearing. They call to mind John Berger's essay 'Why Look at Animals?', about zoos. Looking at buildings, especially in architectural magazines, strikes me as having much in common with the kind of spectating which Berger describes in relation to animals.

Photography serves to domesticate architecture. The published specimens are the Crufts Best in Show, the pedigree chums, as opposed to the feral mongrels that prowl on every street.

a Garry Winogrand, *Untitled ,c.1963*

Take two photographs by Garry Winogrand. First (a), a zoo keeper squeegeeing the tank of a white whale, its seemingly smiling face

traversed by his wiper blade as it swims past inside its aquarium. The zoo keeper is silhouetted against the tank, caught in an equivocal spatial condition: simultaneously excluded, from the whale's domain, and included, within the picture frame established by Winogrand's camera. The zoo keeper's right-armed gesture – the application of blade to glass surface – confirms the transparent membrane as a solid boundary, enclosing many tons of fluid.

b Garry Winogrand, *Los Angeles Airport*

Second (b): a night scene in an American airport in the early sixties. Three passengers are slumped in various postures on fixed seating inside an almost-deserted departure lounge. Beyond them, through the aperture of floor-to-ceiling glazing, we see a jumbo, not an elephant but a plane, pressing its nose against the window pane. It too, like the dolphin, seems to have a smile on its face, the way aeroplanes are anthropomorphised in commercials and cartoons to look like cheerful birds. But maybe it's the smile of smugness: of looking in, on the humans who this time are the creatures in captivity, waiting to be let out, on board, airborne and away.

These two images say a lot to me about

architecture, and how it contains us, and why it is so resilient to photography. The fish tank and the departure lounge. Being kept in and being shut out. And where are we, the viewers, in relation to these places?

Architectural photography prepares you only for the optimum condition, not just the building new-born, pristine, but the building severed neatly from its surroundings, the building always sunbathing, the building in its warmest hues, smiling for the camera. You come to a building knowing it only from its published representation, and there are surprises, always. The deceits of scale, context, and physical condition are instantly unmasked. Usually, instead of glowing – the sheen of the page enhancing its fresh-wiped look – a building simply stands there, locked into a place. And that place is different from the crispness of the margins surrounding it on the page. Shorn of its caption, denuded of the warm thicket of type that settles it into an argument, the building tells you nothing about how you should think about it. Confronted by the actual object, you have to make your own mind up about the nature of the beast.

The life of an architecture critic is a strange one; that of the architectural photographer even stranger, akin to the wildlife observer, permanently on safari. Both set out to find a building – travelling perhaps several thousand miles to stalk this private house, that new museum – so as to bring it home, to be stuffed and mounted on the page, packaged for architects' perusal. Of course, it is possible to tell a story based on plans, sections, and transparencies taken by others. But there are losses, sensations that photographs efface.

I try not to write about buildings I haven't

een in the flesh. My flesh, since theirs is organic, sometimes stone, or timber, or porcelain-enamelled aluminium, attached to a skeleton of steel or a carcass of concrete. To now a building means to have approached it, walked around it, passed through its hambers, felt the light come through, the gravity-denying bounce of the computer boring, the chill of a metal handrail, the xture of a bush-hammered surface, the ound of footfalls on stone steps, the hushed oulence of a lift-cabin lined in American nerry. And noticed the way the receptionist eers up from behind her smooth granite-pped console to ask if she can help. 'No, e just come to have a look...'

The photographer, who usually comes along ter, installs himself (for most, like architects, e male) with tripods and lenses and filters d flash, and makes a different kind of sessment from the writer. Over hours or ys – especially if rain stops play – he gets inhabit the building, at least temporarily, in way that the writer, scrawling notes on the ove in a spiral-bound pad, scarcely does. e photographer takes bearings, plots what ne of day to capture each facade for the ost flattering light. He waits for the sun to st pleasing shadows. He looks for certain ads of relationship between forms, how aces and objects will convert to a mpelling arrangement through the wfinder, and hence on the plane of the ge. He gets in ahead of the opening date, the occupants are not yet admitted, or nerwise they're banished, in order not to ve a messy blur, in long exposures. Rooms e unlocked for him, spaces sealed off while s at work.

he writer wanders around, making sense the building's interlocking sections, ntally joining up spaces that lie in mutual oblivion – like compartments on a Cluedo board – upon the floorplans. The writer spots allusions to other buildings, historic references and private jokes played for the benefit only of other architects in the know. Standing outside, counting columns, or watching the window mullions make highways to heaven, the writer notes how the building forms and reforms into new perspectives with a pace to the right or the left.

But for the photographer, camera in hand, the 'best' position soon makes itself apparent, though it may mean standing in the middle of the road to dodge a lamp-post, or climbing to the umpteenth storey of the building across the way, a vantage-point from which to lift the specimen out of its earth-bound anchorage and into a new and commanding prominence. Never mind that everybody else can only see the building from ground level, or at best, from the top of a double-decker bus; once reproduced, that image from the undisclosed lookout will become the standard view, the authorised 'take', the truth against which other views will seem irredeemably poor approximations.

With light sources balanced, and parallels vertical, the 'official' photos reveal territory to which the ordinary mortal is not privy. The recherché external vantage and the unoccupied interior are corollaries of architecture's split personality: the outer skin, available for viewing, versus the inner sanctum, visible only by appointment. The 'truth' which architectural journals deliver often seems arid by comparison to the life the building leads *in situ*. And by that I mean not just the life that goes on inside, which architectural photography systematically evacuates, but also the spontaneous responses of passers-by.

c Janet Abrams, *Norton House*

Take the Norton House, on Venice Beach, California, designed by Frank Gehry for a screenwriter who has a fondness for the raised platforms from which lifeguards survey swimmers in the broad blue ocean. The structure out front has a kookiness that demands attention: the screenwriter's work-cabin stands on a one-legged support, like a flamingo at rest, with 'eyelid' sunshades, tilted at assorted angles in a strange echo of the old leaves hanging on adjacent palm trees.

Almost everyone who passes the Norton House falters as they push the pram, pedal their bike, or roller-skate along the prom. I take a string of shots (c) capturing these moments of arrest by architecture: broken

78

strides, half-turned heads, outstretched arms pointing out this friendly interruption of the norm. These are not the kind of images which get much published. They have to do with other people, beside the owner, taking possession of a building for a few moments, letting it lodge in their memory of a warm afternoon beside the Pacific.

The single image which sums up the Norton House, oft-reproduced, is precisely the inverse of what onlookers see. Looking from the house towards the water through the screenwriter's cabin, this photograph purports to grant admission to a space expressly sequestered for a single user. The rest of us gain access only at one remove: flicking the pages of the journals, or watching a 'show'n'tell' lecture in which 35mm slides, coupled on a white screen, bring non-contiguous places into adjacency – truffles of built form, scattered around the globe, waiting to be foraged.

The screenwriter's room is empty, so we can peer in undistracted by his person. We are offered *his* view, or close to it, and are left free to guess what goes on in there, to own vicariously, to take a time-share of the optic. And this, after all, is what so compels about architectural photography: we are invited to fill it up with our own speculations, to supply our own designs for living.

In the magazine office, summer 1990, awaiting a courier-delivery of trannies. We have been promised first rights – no other British publication will get to publish these images of X's latest building before us. Effectively, that could mean we'll be the *only* magazine here to cover it, since once a building has been published by one journal, it's quickly regarded as yesterday's soggy muesli by all the others. In other words, it ceases to exist. Happily, the worldwide superfluity of architectural magazines ensures that almost any 'major work' will get plenty of column inches, internationally speaking.

The transparencies arrive. They're only dupes – please can we have the originals? Laid out on the light box, they're like a jigsaw puzzle of stained glass. Like restorers of Mycenæan pottery, we try to reconstruct the building, backwards, from these *Blade Runner* fake-snake scales, these surface chippings from an object on the other side of the globe. Has *A+U* published it, in Japan? At least then there might be something to go by. Nobody here has seen it *in situ*. We resolve to write an extended picture caption based on this second-hand encounter.

The Art Director shunts the images around the light box, cogitating over which to enlarge across the opening double-page spread. Which *one* image will stop the readers in their tracks – in purely photogenic terms? This will not necessarily be the photo that conveys most about the architectural idea. But, what does that mean, 'architectural' when 3-D is already flattened to two? The frontier of inquiry shifts, silently, imperceptibly, across that porous divide between architecture and graphic design.

We put together a narrative, supplemented by some eyewitness commentary by

members of that exclusive club which one (Rem Koolhaas) has dubbed 'the circus of the perpetually jet-lagged' – architects who try to beat the clock of life by travelling backwards round the globe, snaring spare hours as they leapfrog time zones. The words are convincing; the picture spread attractive.

It comes as little surprise when, some weeks later, X calls to let us know we've printed half the photos backwards...

Architectural photography, when confined to black and white, has been principally concerned with such formalistic issues as the nature of the facade, and the building in its context, especially shown in low two-point perspective – the 'Detroit Front Three-Quarters' as photographer Richard Bryant calls this angle, close to the headlight, in homage to car photographers' favourite cliché. But colour: what could that add to the catalogue of impressions?

Rummaging through back copies of *Progressive Architecture*, my attention keeps being drawn to a certain kind of photograph. Not so much an angle of vision as an image which exudes a particularly exotic fragrance, an aroma for the eyes – like the perfumes which leak from the lacquered pages of *Vanity Fair*. This shot I call 'The Twilight Zone', and it deserves the status of an archetype. Irrespective of the type of building thus shown, it seems to have emerged in the 1980s as an obligatory view, a canonic use of colour, as essential to the repertoire of architectural 'poses' as the cake-cutting scene is to every wedding album.

In 'The Twilight Zone' the building has an ethereal glow. It has the surreal lighting of petrochemical plants whose putrid vapours sneak in as you drive past along the freeway, though the air vents are sealed and the windows tightly wound. The building is photographed at night, but rarely against a background of true pitch darkness: set in an urban context, its neighbours contribute random punchcard pinpricks of illumination, while car tail-lights bleed in meandering snail trails – testimony to prolonged exposure.

In such circumstances, the subject of the shot must glow that much more brightly in order to stand out. It does so by virtue of its distinctive plumage: the building (whatever its surface colouring) is washed with amber, aquamarine, mauvy-blue, the sky tinged with the rose of sunset after a perfect cloudless day. We have seen this shot before, but not in the realm of architecture. Its supersaturated hues provide a clue.

It is the holy icon of the space programme: the countdown, where floodlights strafe the shuttle's hull, still clasped by the arms of its support-derrick; the blast-off, with fuel energy turned to blinding light and, soon thereafter, billowing smoke. The photograph serves to make permanent that one moment of hyper-readiness for action – precision-timed, all-systems-go – that split-second vortex towards which months and years of human effort have been funnelled. The building, photographed this way, becomes indelibly inscribed with its crowning moment of technological perfection; no subsequent interpretation can undermine

d John Donat, *Willis, Faber and Dumas Building, Ipswich*

its varnished truth.

Not surprising, then, that many of the buildings first depicted thus belonged to the 'high tech' school, though it is no longer the exclusive visual hallmark. Perhaps it was John Donat's view of Norman Foster's Willis, Faber and Dumas building (d) that started the ball rolling: what by day was a reflective curtain wall of black glass panels dissolved by night to reveal the hidden interior – floor slabs, columns, suspended ceiling, mechanical services, all exposed as an immaculate conception.

Subsequently, for buildings by Norman Foster and by Richard Rogers such shots have come to be an essential element of the 'public image'. Think of Foster's Hong Kong and Shanghai Bank (e), or of Rogers' Lloyd's

e Richard Bryant, *Hong Kong and Shanghai Bank, Hong Kong, 1985*

London insurance headquarters, and 'The
light Zone' images spring instantly to mind.
visible from the architecture, the
otographic representation becomes the
ans by which the building is circulated,
ced in geo-synchronous orbit. In short, a
ot which connotes nativity, the birth of a
lding, its launch into outer space.
or buildings by other architects, such as
hard Meier, this type of image takes to an
reme the modernist credo of external
ibility: that the outside should give clear
pression of what is going on within. The
TO dusk shots of Meier museums –
pecially the Atlanta High and the Frankfurt
corative Arts museums – transform the
ationship of transparent to opaque
faces. Glazed and grid-panelled portions
e reversed out in evocation of Magritte's
rie Brussels streetscapes where a bright
y and darkened buildings – lit from within –

Johnson, *Inmos Microprocessor Factory, Newport -
ral spine*, acrylic on canvas, 1985

t day and night in impossible co-existence.
e solid structure of Meier's buildings is
ade to appear less a boundary enclosing
ace, than a cage, a silhouette of bars, with
dded window mullions acting as dainty
rtcullises to restrain some incandescent
-force inside.
his same kind of messianic glow informs
e 'classic' interior shot of Richard Rogers's
nos building. A view down the central
cess corridor, it was subsequently
hanced – in terms of its mechanistic sheen
y Ben Johnson's 1985 photo-realist
nting (f) from exactly the same position,
king through paired glass doors. Johnson

dvertisement for Minolta

h Advertisement for London Electricity Board, 1988/9

tidies up the reflections on the floor surface,
and pares away at the details until his image
becomes the sincerest form of flattery: even
more perfect than the photograph, while
subtly hinting at the latter's insufficient
artifice.

But the Lloyd's Building occupies a different
atmospheric level, surpassing all others in its
chameleon fecundity. Untethered by the
gravity of its Leadenhall Street location, this
paragon of 'high tech' leads a promiscuous
life in adverts, and on magazine covers and
book jackets (g). Immediately after its
completion, during the latter 1980s, it began
to be appropriated as *the* ready reference for
'the cutting edge'. Whether the product was
computers, cars, airlines, or international
courier services, the Lloyd's Building was
there basking in the background, the
Madonna of architecture, muscle-bound and
floodlit, exuding an air of technological

prowess.

The prosaic-seeming London Electricity
Board borrowed some of the building's
glamour, parking an LEB van in front of the
effulgent north facade, on one of its customer
service leaflets (h). Atmospherically blurred
(the city as seen by the Man on the Move) but
with its vertebrae-like stair towers still
recognisable, the Lloyd's Building even lent
itself to advertise SERPS, the State Earnings-
Related Pension Scheme. Irrespective of the
ongoing controversy about its interior
functioning and actual, rather than supposed,
technological innovations, its visual mix of
anthropomorphism and unadulterated science
fiction made it a uniquely powerful symbol of
the Future Perfect, here and now – an Eiffel
Tower for our times.

In 1983, Saatchi and Saatchi produced a
90-second TV commercial for British Airways,
entitled *Manhattan Landing*, in which the island
of New York, appears, *Close Encounters*-
style, in the blackened sky over London. It
hovers over the heads of stunned onlookers,
before descending into Heathrow Airport in a
deft conflation of departure point and
destination. No UFO this: signature
skyscrapers, particularly the World Trade
Centre's twin peaks, identify this ball of fire
incontrovertibly as Manhattan. The ad implied
that, instead of having to catch a plane to get
to somewhere else, British Airways brings the
world to you, architecture all-inclusive. This is
the rhetoric of 'The Twilight Zone', the inflight-
magazine look which renders all kinds of
buildings, in all kinds of places, fundamentally
interchangeable. As easily relocated as – with
the twist of a scalpel blade or the click of a
mouse – a photo on a page.

Since that commercial was screened,
Manhattan has landed in London, or at least a
phantom version thereof: at Canary Wharf. In
parallel with the change of architectural mood
during the latter 1980s, a discernible shift
occurred in the preferred style of
representation. Instead of whetting appetites

i *Terry Farrell Partnership, Alban Gate*, from letting brochure, 1987/8

j Carl Laubin, *London Bridge City scheme, painting, 1988*

for new developments using colour photomontages, architects of a neo-classical persuasion eschewed the photo-mechanical image, and rehabilitated the oil painting as the means of conveying a halcyon era yet-to-come. What photographers John Donat and Richard Einzig were to a previous generation, painter Carl Laubin has become for the present. His lovingly detailed *mises-en-scène* indulge in a freedom to fictionalise that photomontage, with its inbuilt implications of advanced technology, cannot achieve.

Compare the montage of Terry Farrell's Alban Gate office towers (i) with the painted perspective of John Simpson's London Bridge City scheme (j), produced only a few years apart in the late 1980s. The former inserts an architectural model of the building-to-come –

photographed from the correct angle and appropriate 'distance', under the right light – into a London cityscape as it is. The illusion is of a building of the future, ripe and ready for immediate occupation.

The Laubin painting, by contrast, offers not just the building already there, but the building having-been-there-a-long-time-already. It speaks to a yearning for some other kind of future, one which recuperates an imagined better past, in which 'newness' is not valued as an index of 'progress'. Rather, buildings arrive instantly weathered, like broken-in brogues. Excessively populated by costumed 'gentlefolk', and rendered in the dulcet colours of an everlasting Bank Holiday, Laubin's paintings suggest that the buildings depicted will regenerate that cherished aspect

of the public realm – street life – which modernist architecture so singularly failed to sustain, and possibly even destroyed.

But in both modes of representation, photomontage and painting alike, the disruption of construction, and the traumas adjustment to a new visual feature are equa skipped over. Either kind will do for the lettin brochure, an archetype of the 1980s which (like the tourist guide) emphasises selected 'highlights' of a locale while dispensing altogether with its problematic underside. Architectural photography too is defined by exclusions: the unsightly, the failed, the rain soaked, the crumbling and abandoned.

So what are these glamorous photos for? The same could be asked of the buildings. Landmarks, they advertise the cultural sophistication of the people who commissioned them, and by extension, of the places where they're located. As Martin Pawley has argued, 'architecture – whether megastructural or contextual – has lost its c art-historical identity, but gains instead the status of a fixed opportunity inducement. If it is successful it will multiply the attractions of a city by the way in which its image is reproduced all over the world. The true success or failure of a city is no longer physical but conceptual in a way that depen upon its global economic propaganda.' (*Blueprint*, March 1991)

Photography is certainly complicit in that propaganda, an essential weapon in the worldwide battle for urban prestige. But Pawley pushes his proposition *ad absurdum* for the cities we live in are surely more than mere conglomerations of competing visual myths. The risk is that our perception of the built environment could come to rest on images alone, and that such surrogates mig be taken to construct an experience more persuasive, more enchanted, than the physical – and social – world we actually inhabit.

PHOTOGRAPHING ARCHITECTURE PETER GREENAWAY

I have, on more than one occasion, been accused of wasting actors in the interests of praising architecture. 'Why employ such talent if all you want is an architectural manikin, a scale figure for a facade, a body to measure off a curving space?' However, I am pleased to now know three actors, self–consciousness permitting, who are happy to sit in front of a fine piece of architecture and clap it if it pleases them, exactly like the architectural enthusiasts clapping the Roman Pantheon in the film *The Belly of an Architect*. The architecture, in these three cases, was, not surprisingly, the Taj Mahal, more surprisingly a Wrexham gasometer and most disturbingly, anything by Quinlan Terry – you may create the habit, but there is no telling the outcome.

I enjoy the excitements of photographing architecture and architectural spaces, though the camera must be, for me, a movie camera. On the face of it, this might seem to demand a different set of pictorial values than filming the world with a stills camera, but there are contradictions and paradoxes and not a few prejudices. Here are a few prejudices that shout loudly. Moving pictures do not necessarily have to move, and I like to employ a camera that is pleased to find a frame and stay still, loathe to move without some very pressing reason. And that reason, as like as not, might very well not be narrative. I feel sympathetic to a camera that will not be a slave to an actor, and has no itch to follow him if he makes a move to leave the screen. Rather than examine the hair in his nostrils, I would, as soon as not, prefer to watch the relationship of his body to the ceiling above his head or the wall at his back. Mixing Bernini with Newton, it is also appropriate, I might

say, to have an exaggerated respect for gravity. 'Gravity is the best thing to happen to an architect, since in fixing his feet to the ground, it permits his head to remain in the clouds'. A third consideration is that although you may move, architecture will not. A fourth consideration is that the human eye-level, give or take eight inches, is a constant five foot four inches from the ground. A fifth, sixth and seventh reason is that the cinema, despite searching out Schwarzenegger's breasts and Madonna's buttocks, Cher's lingerie and the deck of the USS Enterprise, is not often truly interested in corporeality, stuffs and sculptural spaces. Which is a pity. The architectural photographer, more than likely, is. Is there much true interest in the cinema in architecture for its own sake? Happily I would say often. We can all mention a favourite. For me, Tisse photographing tenements for Eisenstein's *Strike*; Muller photographing New Orleans for Jarmusch's *Down by Law*; Coutard looking at Godard's Paris, especially and unexpectedly its tourist monuments; Fellini looking at Rome; Woody Allen looking at Manhattan, with special reference to that architectural lesson in *Hannah and her Sisters*, and top of the list, two great directors of location architecture – Resnais and Antonioni, with Sacha Vierny and Gianni di Venanzo as cameramen.

There is a sequence in Resnais's *Providence* of Bogarde taking a trip in a sleek, slow-moving car along a street of bourgeois buildings, middle-class palaces and ivy-covered domestic mausoleums. The sequence is accompanied by the most proud and celebratory music. Narratively slight, unaccountably disturbing, I have rarely looked at comparable buildings without experiencing

an exciting disquiet. And I am convinced the provocation is dependent on the viewing of that certain architecture, and not on the Gielgud voice-over. Resnais is always a super evoker of drama through architecture, and s⦾ is never far away, whether it is in the provincial, collaborationist, gloomy streets o⦾ Nevers in *Hiroshima Mon Amour* or the sunse⦾ casinos in *Muriel* or that most disturbing of sensuous architectural nightmare-dreams, *La Year in Marienbad*, where the slumbering building at the centre of that black and white film is its true, major and very colourful protagonist. Perhaps we should also not forget Resnais's dry depiction of the walls an⦾ huts and concrete posts of the concentration camps in *Night and Fog*, the very first filmic essay on the Holocaust, where warm corporeality had long deceased, turning its inmates into only stuffs in an architectural space.

I remember a small incident in Antonioni's *L'Avventura*. With some shame and some jealousy, the pathetic lover spitefully knocks over a student's inkwell to flood an architectural drawing. Antonioni trained to be an architect, but became a film-maker instead From *L'Avventura* to *Blow-Up* by way of *La Notte*, *The Eclipse* and *Red Desert* and then *Passenger*, there is sureness of how to see his people against shiny walls and dead brick bright sunlit roof-tops and melancholic, end-o⦾ the-day street–corners. His superb atmospheric architectural montages say muc⦾ about the characters who always evade straight description, an irritation to some wh⦾ persist in rationalising so much that the architectural poetry is too often brought low by journalistic cliché, like insisting the water towers in *The Eclipse* are a symbol for the H-

nb mushroom cloud – making simple literal
anings from complex architectural
xience. London in *Blow-Up* was full of newly-
erved domestic streets photographed to
as still and dangerous as those Magritte
ssels houses at lamp-lighting time.
know for certain that my enthusiasms for
icting architecture on film have arrived via
ting, from an excitement for the simplest
most vestigial representation of
hitecture with a Mantegna Sebastian
ached to a composite column, to the
ssed crowds filling the architectural spaces
Veronese. The film *The Draughtsman's
ntract*, intimately reflecting its own subject
structure, began for me three years
ore the camera turned, in a garden on the
sh border, where I methodically and
nstakingly drew the shifting shadows
oss the facade of a Victorian house. The
ade was a very different pictorial
position at morning, noon and night, and
excitements of depicting the play of a light
a crisply defined building have persisted.
location house for *The Draughtsman's
ntract* had suffered the softening of
torian husbandry and twentieth century
weniences. It was the camera's
ponsibility to turn back the clock and at
st prepare a ground that was in tune with
received opinions of a historical period of
ometric gardens and formal decorative
haviour with framings carefully chosen to
ncur with authorities from the topographical
ff to the constipated Devis. Photography of
countryhouse is almost a sub-genre,
pealing to a much scrambled notion of
stalgia, snobbery and fantasy of a pre-
ctric rural idyll that has provided much work
many cameramen, inside and outside the

cinema, though perhaps none have been so
atmospherically successful as Atget at
Versailles and Saint Cloud.

To photograph and to film architecture is to
become swiftly aware of multiple curiosities of
vision, of excessive optical illusion and
downright retinal deceptions. If your favoured
architectural setting is classical or neo-
classical, then you have to contend with the
frustrating mutability of verticals that persist in
pretending to be diagonals, in the refusal of
carefully stage-managed entasis to work for
the camera lens and to have to contend with
bending and fluctuating horizontals in every
wide-shot. The demands of a cinematic
narrative and the necessity to keep an actor's
respect for, and reliance on, gravity, mean
accommodation, and the precisely envisaged
filming of the architectural space has to be
jeopardised, for not every film can shoot its
architectural verticals on the angle like Reed's
The Third Man. In paying homage to
architectural painting, and in trying,
occasionally, to understand what a painter saw
and how he saw it – say Canaletto painting
Venice or Saenredam painting an Amsterdam
church, or Piranesi drawing Rome or Monet
looking at Chartres Cathedral, or even Sickert
painting Camden Town – is to realise how
much a painter of architecture can cheat with
his multiple vanishing points, his cavalier
regard for scale, his apparently arbitrary
palette, his ubiquitous vision that can see –
with apparent conviction – both sides of the
same wall at once. However much a painter
cheats within his very agreeable legitimate
licenses, it is not to say that the architect has
not cheated before him. With Sacha Vierny,
the director of photography on five pictures, I
have come to believe that, in terms of

classical perfection, the architect, or perhaps
it is his builder, has often severely erred in his
consideration of proportions. For the camera –
which of course never lies – refuses to agree
that the spot chosen by the architect as the
centre of all things, is not necessarily, given
the perspectives, the correct one.

Architectural excitements cannot be
separated from the excitements of light. In the
film *A Zed and Two Noughts*, much of the
background architecture was the Hollywood-
Dutch Art Deco of van Ravenstyn who built
Rotterdam Zoo in three years and, unusually,
all of a piece, from the hippopotamus house to
an Eric Gill Diana chasing deer along the
parapet of the aviary. At night, through the
camera, the architecture seemed to be newly
minted and lion and tiger prowled with
beautiful incongruity among the softly moulded
edges and irresponsible filigree. In daylight
though all the camera persisted in seeing was
the decay of rusting bars and the stucco
falling off the rococo concrete balustrades.
Architecture after dark is almost a genre in
itself with a singularly curious rule that, for
once, the camera can easily see what the
human eye cannot – except perhaps by the
light of a wartime explosion or the flare of a
firework display. That celebrated train-spotter,
O. Winston Link, setting out to trap fast-
moving locomotives in the blink of a startled
eye, also trapped small town railway
architecture, throwing the brightest of light
uniquely into front porches and dead-of-night
sitting-rooms, lighting up forgotten cornices
and spare bedrooms.

Sacha Vierny and I paced and re-paced
selected buildings in Rome on the film *The
Belly of an Architect*, to find the exact required
emphasis of man and building. We never found

84

it with the impossibly sited Augusteum which refused to permit its totality to be seen in any conceivable wide-shot, but maybe the Pantheon and the Victor Emmanuel Building were more lenient and some sense of their bulk was imprisoned on the celluloid. The latter, distastefully nicknamed 'the Emmanuella', and referred to as 'the wedding-cake' because of its glinting, dazzling icing-sugar finish or as 'the typewriter' for its likeness to a giant twenties Olivetti portable, is nonetheless most advantageously placed. From its sweeping balcony, cracking up through hasty building, you could see seven hills and twenty-one Roman architectural masterpieces.

Filming the Emmanuella was full of imponderables, how to make a retreat far enough back to appreciate the whole scale but without excessive loss of detail. A close approach loses the theatrical relationship of the whole to the bright sky that gives its edges such a hard-line sharpness, and a very close view gives only a gallery of detail that could possibly be found on any Beaux-Arts neo-classical fantasy. Downstairs in the Emanuella's deep basement are all the rejected entries for the competition to decide the building's architect – over five hundred huge, mouldering plaster models. I would have liked to have photographed them all, if only to emphasise what the Roman producers themselves tried to tell me – no doubt in gentle mockery at the presumption of an outsider coming to Rome to photograph their equivocally appreciated building – that the architect threw himself from the roof in pique at being poorly appreciated even though he was the winner. An apocryphal story, repeated of the architect of the Taj Mahal, Sacré Coeur and Ely Cathedral. Three photographers have fallen off the Empire State Building, two off the Statue of Liberty and one off Mount Rushmore.

After studying Piranesi's efforts to place the Pantheon in its own huge space, when the camera was lifted onto its tracks to film the building for The Belly of an Architect, the enclosing piazza most definitely closed in further. Piranesi had cheated more expertly than we could ever cheat. From eye–level, any attempt to relate this fine building to Plato's bold architectural solids of perfection proved too difficult, if it was imperative also that the film's narrative characteristics were to be respected, and at night watching the circle of the moon rise above the triangle of the tympanum above the square of the portico. A compromising retreat would put the camera-dolly deep inside the hamburger-parlour opposite the Pantheon's atrium and our presence in there was certainly an irritating focus for an architectural heritage abused. It brought forth fresh arguments of the architect's responsibility which I was keen to think might be one of the themes of the film.

The whole film of The Belly of an Architect was photographed as though the cameraman himself was a classical architect, whose disciplines were obsessively related to the flat, formal, symmetrical plan, the scrupulously scaled elevation, and the frontal set-square-conscious facade. To film the large, vulnerable chubby body of Brian Dennehy up against

those sharp edges and huge expanses of gridded marble was to emphasise the contrasting scale and durability of both. Possible immortality against certain mortality. The colour scheme of the film was arranged to aid the same. Roman architectural colours, terracotta, cream, white, burnt sienna, yellow ochre and deep black shadows from a directly overhead sun were permissible. Green and blue, the dominant colours of nature, were to be eliminated by filters and judicious framing. This was to be a man-made landscape. These Roman colours are also the colours of a healthy human body. Green, the colour of the maturing corpse, was the hero's enemy. When the architect plunges to his self-prepared death, his back broken on a green car, the rigorous horizontal and vertical classical format is slashed by a compositional diagonal that screams against the formality of all this excessive regimentation. Curiously of course it was very easy to frame and film that diagonal from a peaceful, spacious traffic island, whereas the formal classicism with its exacting symmetry inevitably placed the camera in the centre of the road in a Roman rush-hour.

Three photographers were encouraging for two sets of ideas in the film Drowning by Numbers: Hilla and Bernd Becher for the water-towers and Meyerowitz for the beach-houses. What better symbol for a film of drowning than a water-tower, hoisting so much water over the heads of the protagonists? There are three towers in the film, one for each drowning, a small list beside the Becher hundreds. I had photographed water-ttowers along the Humber in earlier films, perverting their purposes, imagining they had been converted into echoic film-vaults, having in their blunt circularity, much sympathetic resemblance to a stack of empty film cans that clanged when kicked. Meyerowitz's white frame, damp-floored beach-houses variously photographed in conditions of thunderstorm or bright noon-light spawned a canvas-sailed pavilioned beach-house from the art department of the film, that pleased and entertained so much that prints from the film-frame were demanded by German and American viewers, thinking perhaps that from appearances they too could build themselves such a country cabin or seaside gazebo. Our building, pasteboard to the winds of the North Sea, blew right away on the night of that famous October hurricane of '87.

Avoiding the inconvenience of the unobtainable vantage-point and the uncooperative weather, there is the minor European painting genre of the architectural capriccio. Put your favourite building in a location of your own choosing, mix up the chronologies and styles, build a utopian city of immaculate perspectives like Piero della Francesca's Ideal Town, put St Pauls on the Grand Canal and Cologne Cathedral on the Hudson. Piranesi must be the most pre-eminent exponent, though Monsu Desiderio for me is more mysterious and Etienne-Louis Boullée more monumental. The English were keen not only to buy the architectural fantasies of Claude and Poussin and Hubert Robert, but also to try and build them to entertain a guest

as an incident on a Saturday afternoon walk. Delightfully, you can prefabricate the same architectural excitements in cinema, in a studio, with an armoury of devices – glass-painting; multiple light-sources; blue-screen backgrounds; trompe l'oeil artifices. And ligh and colour them to the most exacting specifications. Architecture built solely for the camera. At noon you can make dawn, and after lunch, you can make midnight, with a moon that can be manipulated to shine right into the peristyle and separate out seven separate shadows from seven separate pillar Such delightful extravagances were used on the film The Cook, The Thief, His Wife and He Lover – building a series of large architectura spaces to support the notion of consumer excess, cannibalism and eating-out. Some sa in the huge spaces of this extended restaurant, a travelling history of architecture From left to right, the camera on rails moved from the blue Stonehenge exterior to green Piranesi 'Krak des Chevaliers' medievalism to vulgar Beaux–Arts Baroque to a Modernist bathroom complete with Bauhaus fittings. On possible at the movies? Not necessarily so. For in any capital city in Europe, walking dow the once-ancient and now-modern main stree you may very well observe that chronological change. Besides, the restaurant trade are ideal pasticheurs, eager to quickly assemble atmosphere to match the food.

We have travelled several stages further in photographing these hedonistic architectural delights in the film Prospero's Books, a version of Shakespeare's The Tempest. Prospero is able, as with Ellis at Portmerion o Hadrian at his famous villa, to magically summon any architectural substance and buil it into a personal capriccio. We have borrowe the Bomarzo Mouth of Hell, the Roman pyramid of Cestius, a little of Bernini's St Peter's colonnade and an Istanbul Turkish Bath, and modelled a palace for Prospero tha repeats in theory, the idea of the Christian church trapped inside the Great Mosque at Cordoba – a place so architecturally astonishing that the claim 'There is nothing crueller in life than to be blind in Cordoba' is, a little excitable, a possibility to be considered. But the architectural highlight of Prospero's palaces is a to-scale reconstructic in wood and plaster, instead of stone and stucco, of Michelangelo's superb vestibule to the Laurenziana library in Florence seen as Michelangelo could never have seen it, with the fourth wall removed so that a viewer can stand back from that tight space and view the cool symmetries with an omnipotent eye. I have yet to see a still photograph of that magnificent but awkward space that does it any reasonable justice. So, do not just take your own camera to the architecture, bring your architecture to the camera.

However, there are melancholic necessities The buildings for the camera have to come down, be dismantled. All the scenes in Michelangelo's wood and plaster Laurenziana had to be filmed in one day and then the clou capped towers, the gorgeous palaces, the solemn temples had to be removed. This sad imperative has spawned a new project – The Stairs – a film that will never be a film, but a series of architectural sets, ten gallery spaces around the world to hold a deliberation on the mutability of film, where the cheat of the false perspective, the disorientation of invented scales, the curse of having always to make a choice, the wish to use thirty light-readings on one architectural view, the wish to see an architectural facade ten times throughout its history of decay – all these and more, without the limiting necessity of the anecdotes of plot and the vanity of actors will be made explicit ... and then the camera can restfully contemplate the excitements of architecture to its heart's delight.

LIST OF WORKS

All dimensions are given with height preceding width

Berenice Abbott (USA b.1898)
Rockefeller Center, 1932
toned silver gelatine print
254 x 203 mm
Lent by Marlborough Graphics, London

Foundations of Rockefeller Center, 1932
silver gelatine print (modern print)
330 x 254 mm
Lent by Marlborough Graphics, London

Steel Girders (Rockefeller Center), 1932
silver gelatine print (modern print)
343 x 267 mm
Lent by Marlborough Graphics, London

Exchange Place, New York, c.1934
silver gelatine print
493 x 140 mm
Lent by Chris Taylor, London

Flatiron Building, 1938
silver gelatine print
340 x 265 mm
Lent by The Photographers' Gallery Print Room, London

Erich Angenendt (Germany 1894-1962)
Half-timbering, 1952
silver gelatine print
282 x 374 mm
Lent by the Museum Folkwang, Essen

Jean-Eugène-Auguste Atget (France 1857-1927)
The Corner of Rue Valette and The Pantheon, 1925
limited edition albumen print produced by MOMA, New York
(modern print)
180 x 238 mm
Lent by a private collector

Lewis Baltz (USA b.1945)
West Wall, Unoccupied Industrial Structure, 20 Airway Drive,
Costa Mesa
element 45 from The New Industrial Parks Near Irvine,
California, 1974
silver gelatine print
153 x 229 mm
Lent by The Museum of Fine Arts, Houston; museum
purchase with funds provided by the National Endowment for
the Arts and Gamma Phi Beta

Construction Detail, East Wall Xerox, 1821 Dyer Road, Santa
Ana
element 27 from The New Industrial Parks Near Irvine,
California, 1974
silver gelatine print
153 x 229 mm
Lent by The Museum of Fine Arts, Houston; museum
purchase with funds provided by the National Endowment for
the Arts and Gamma Phi Beta

Olivo Barbieri (Italy b.1954)
Hong Kong, 1989
C-type print
275 x 552 mm
Lent by the artist

Hong Kong, Happy Valley, 1989
C-type print
275 x 552 mm
Lent by the artist

Hong Kong, Happy Valley, 1989
C-type print
275 x 552 mm
Lent by the artist

Hong Kong, Kowloon, 1989
C-type print
275 x 552 mm
Lent by the artist

Suzhou, China 1989
C-type print
275 x 552 mm
Lent by the artist

Gabriele Basilico (Italy b.1944)
Dunkerque Harbour,1984
(from a project commissioned by Mission Photographique
de la DATAR, 1984)
silver gelatine print
400 x 500 mm
Lent by the artist

Dunkerque Harbour, 1984
(from a project commissioned by Mission Photographique de
la DATAR, 1984)
silver gelatine print
400 x 500 mm
Lent by the artist

Dunkerque Harbour, 1984
(from a project commissioned by Mission Photographique de
la DATAR, 1984)
silver gelatine print
400 x 500 mm
Lent by the artist

Dunkerque Harbour, 1984
(from a project commissioned by Mission Photographique de
la DATAR, 1984)
silver gelatine print
400 x 500 mm
Lent by the artist

Herbert Bayer (Austria/USA 1900-85)
View from the Transporter Bridge, Marseille, 1928
silver gelatine print (modern print)
317 x 197 mm
Lent by a private collector

Transporter Bridge, Marseille, 1928
silver gelatine print (modern print)
248 x 168 mm
Lent by Joella Bayer, California

Bernd Becher (Germany b.1931)
Hilla Becher (Germany b. 1934)
Coal Tipple, Goodspring, Philladelphia, c.1970
4 silver gelatine prints
112 x 162 mm each
Lent by the Board of Trustees of the Victoria and Albert
Museum, London

oling Towers, Zeche Waltrop, c.1970
er gelatine print
7 x 300 mm
t by the Board of Trustees of the Victoria and Albert
seum, London

s Holder, Power Station, Essen Karnap, c.1970
er gelatine print
7 x 300 mm
t by the Board of Trustees of the Victoria and Albert
seum, London

for Coal, Big Pit Colliery, South Wales, c.1970
er gelatine print
7 x 300 mm
t by the Board of Trustees of the Victoria and Albert
seum, London

ène Binet (France b. 1959)
e House Without Walls by Daniel Libeskind, Milan Triennale,
86
er gelatine print
5 x 380 mm
nt by the artist

e House Without Walls by Daniel Libeskind, Milan Triennale,
86
er gelatine print
5 x 380 mm
nt by the artist

uis-Auguste Bisson (France 1814-1900)
guste-Rosalie Bisson (France 1826-1900)
eims Cathedral, West Front, Portals, c.1855-60
umen print
2 x 370 mm
nt by the Board of Trustees of the Victoria and Albert
useum, London

argaret Bourke-White (USA 1904-71)
e Loading Docks, Superior, Wisconsin, 1929
er gelatine print (facsimile print produced by Life Picture
rvice, New York)
6 x 279 mm
Margaret Bourke-White, Life Magazine & Time Warner Inc

Rosenbaum Grain Corporation, 1931
silver gelatine print (modern print)
356 x 279 mm
Lent by Syracuse University Library

Rosenbaum Grain Corporation, 1931
silver gelatine print (facsimile print produced by Syracuse
University Library)
356 x 279 mm

Bill Brandt (UK 1904-83)
Rainswept Roofs, 1930s
silver gelatine print
228 x 198 mm
Lent by Noya Brandt

Richard Bryant (UK b.1947)
Hong Kong and Shanghai Bank Headquarters, Hong Kong,
1985
Cibachrome
610 x 413 mm
Lent by Arcaid, London

Staatsgalerie, Zurich, 1985
Cibachrome
610 x 508 mm
Lent by Arcaid, London

Staatsgalerie, Zurich, 1985
Cibachrome
610 x 508 mm
Lent by Arcaid, London

Lloyds Building, London, 1986
Cibachrome
610 x 508 mm
Lent by Arcaid, London

Vitra Museum, Weil, 1990
Cibachrome
610 x 508 mm
Lent by Arcaid, London

Vitra Museum, Weil, 1990
Cibachrome
610 x 508 mm
Lent by Arcaid, London

Harry Callahan (USA b.1912)
Skyscraper, Chicago, 1953
silver gelatine print
356 x 279 mm
Lent by Pace/MacGill Gallery, New York

New York, 1974
silver gelatine print
154 x 160 mm
Lent by Pace MacGill Gallery, New York

Martin Charles (UK b.1940)
Stansted Airport, 1991
C-type print
508 x 406 mm
Lent by the artist

Stansted Airport, 1991
C-type print
508 x 406 mm
Lent by the artist

Roelof Paul Citroen (Netherlands 1896-1983)
Metropolis, 1923
colour print (facsimile print produced by University of Leiden
Prentenkabinet)
770 x 590 mm
© DACS 1991

William Clift (USA b.1944)
Reflection, Old St Louis County Courthouse, Missouri, 1976
silver gelatine print
356 x 432 mm
Lent by the artist

Alvin Langdon Coburn (UK 1882-1966)
Broadway, New York, 1909/10
photogravure
195 x 104 mm
Lent by The Royal Photographic Society, Bath

Singer Building, New York, 1909/10
photogravure
207 x 62 mm
Lent by The Royal Photographic Society, Bath

Erich Consemüller (Germany 1902-57)
The Building as Stage (New Bauhaus Building), c.1927
silver gelatine print (facsimile print produced by the Bauhaus Archive, Berlin)
310 x 173 mm

John Davies (UK b.1949)
Steel VI, Phase 11, Broadgate, 8 February 1989
silver gelatine print
381 x 571 mm
Lent by the artist

Steel IX, Phase 11, Broadgate, 8 February 1989
silver gelatine print
381 x 571 mm
Lent by the artist

Philip Henry Delamotte (France 1820-89)
Entrance to the Byzantine Court, Crystal Palace, 1850s
albumen print
230 x 280 mm
Lent by the Board of Trustees of the Victoria and Albert Museum, London

Mark Dell (UK 1883-1959)
H.L. Wainwright (UK)
Pioneer Health Centre, Peckham (interior), 1935
silver gelatine print (modern print)
380 x 280 mm
Lent by the Architectural Press, London

Embassy Court, Brighton, 1935
silver gelatine print (facsimile print produced by the Architectural Press, London)
380 x 280 mm

Ramsgate Municipal Airport, 1937
silver gelatine print
325 x 580 mm
Lent by The British Architectural Library Photographs Collection, London

London Electricity Showroom, Regent Street, 1938
silver gelatine print
585 x 410 mm
Lent by The British Architectural Library Photographs Collection, London

Jan Dibbets (Netherlands b.1941)
Three Cupolas, 1989-90
3 photo-collages on screenprinted backgrounds
900 x 900 mm each
Lent by Waddington Graphics, London

John Donat (UK b.1933)
Dunelm House, Durham and Kingsgate Footbridge, 1966
silver gelatine print
305 x 406 mm
Lent by the artist

Boots, Nottingham, 1968
silver gelatine print
305 x 406 mm
Lent by the artist

Habitat, Wallingford, 1974
silver gelatine print
305 x 406 mm
Lent by the artist

Goffs Bloodstock Sales, County Kildare, 1975
silver gelatine print
305 x 406 mm
Lent by the artist

Sainsbury Centre, University of East Anglia, 1978
silver gelatine print
305 x 406 mm
Lent by the artist

Jim Dow (USA b.1942)
Veteran's Stadium, Philadelphia, Pennsylvania, 1980
3 Ektacolour prints
254 x 610 mm
Lent by the artist

Busch Stadium, St Louis, Missouri, 1982
3 Ektacolour prints
254 x 610 mm
Lent by the artist

Tancrède R. Dumas (? Italy ?-1905)
Temple of Jupiter, Baalbek, c.1880s
albumen print
419 x 530 mm
Lent by Ken and Jenny Jacobson, Essex

William Eggleston (USA b.1937)
Greenwood Moose Lodge, 1981
from Southern Suite Portfolio
dye transfer print
252 x 384 mm
Lent by the Board of Trustees of the Victoria and Albert Museum, London

Richard Einzig (UK 1932-80)
Helsinki Concert Hall no 16, 1965
silver gelatine print
508 x 406 mm
Lent by Arcaid, London

History Faculty Building, Cambridge, 1968
silver gelatine print
406 x 508 mm
Lent by Arcaid, London

Pompidou Centre, 1978
silver gelatine print
508 x 406 mm
Lent by Arcaid, London

Frederick Henry Evans (UK 1853-1943)
Stairway in South West Turret, Lincoln Cathedral, 1898
platinum print
197 x 124 mm
Lent by The Royal Photographic Society, Bath

Lincoln Cathedral from the Castle, 1898
photogravure
210 x 159 mm
Lent by The Royal Photographic Society, Bath

'A Sea of Steps', Wells Cathedral, 1903
modern hand-pulled, dust grained photogravure for 'Aperture' 1984
219 x 191 mm
Lent by The Royal Photographic Society, Bath

Walker Evans (USA 1903-75)
Brooklyn Bridge, 1929
silver gelatine print (modern print)
205 x 120 mm
Lent by the Walker Evans Estate, Connecticut
© Walker Evans Estate

Ossining, New York, 1930
silver gelatine print
105 x 198 mm
Lent by a private collector

Scarborough, New York, 1931
silver gelatine print
200 x 155 mm
Lent by a private collector

Furniture Store Sign, near Birmingham, Alabama, 1936
silver gelatine print
180 x 230 mm
Lent by Centre Canadien d'Architecture/Canadian Centre for Architecture, Montréal

Billboard Painters, Florida, 1934
silver gelatine print (modern print)
190 x 242 mm
Lent by the Walker Evans Estate, Conneticut
© Walker Evans Estate

Richard Perkins' Storefront, Moundville, Alabama, 1936
silver gelatine print
200 x 250 mm
Lent by the Board of Trustees of the Victoria and Albert Museum, London

Leo Herbert Felton (UK ?-1968)
Olympia Interior Staircase, 1930
silver gelatine print
555 x 400 mm
Lent by The British Architectural Library Photographs Collection, London

Dudley Penguin Pool, 1937
silver gelatine print
160 x 210 mm
Lent by The British Architectural Library Photographs Collection, London

The Hackney Gazette
The Demolition of Northaird Point, Hackney on 3 November 1985
photograph taken for The Hackney Gazette (photographer, Chris Wood)
610 x 508 mm

John Havinden (UK 1908-87)
Lawn Road Flats, 1934
silver gelatine print
580 x 405 mm
Lent by The British Architectural Library Photographs Collection, London

John Heartfield (Germany 1891-1968)
The Choir of the Arms Industry, 1934
collotype
548 x 390 mm
Lent by the Board of Trustees of the Victoria and Albert Museum, London

Bill Hedrich (USA b.1912)
Bear Run, Fallingwater, 1937
modern print
279 x 356 mm
Lent by the Chicago Historical Society

Window, Fallingwater, 1937
modern print
356 x 279 mm
Lent by the Chicago Historical Society

Hedrich-Blessing Ltd
AT&T Building, Chicago by Adrian Smith (Skidmore, Owings & Merrill) for Stein & Company
computer-generated image produced in 1990 by Digital Transparencies Inc. for Hedrich-Blessing Ltd; photographer Bob Harr
completed image 406 x 305 mm
site shot 305 x 240 mm
model shot 305 x 240 mm

77 West Wacker Drive, Chicago by Ricardo Bofill (Taller de Arquitectura) with Destephano /Goettsch for The Prime Group Inc.
computer-generated image produced in 1990 by Digital Transparencies Inc. for Hedrich-Blessing Ltd; photographer, Bob Shimer
completed image 406 x 305 mm
site shot 305 x 240 mm
model shot 305 x 240 mm

Florence Henri (Switzerland 1893-1982)
Wall through Window, 1930
silver gelatine print
340 x 267 mm
Lent by the Museum Folkwang, Essen

s Hine (USA 1874-1940)
on a Mast, Empire State Building, New York, 1931
 gelatine print
x 279 mm
by fotomann inc, New York

Otto Hoppé (UK 1878-1972)
attan seen through the girders of Brooklyn Bridge, New
1919
ide print
x 230 mm
by The Royal Photographic Society, Bath

ar Hörl (Germany b.1950)
Grosse Vertikale II, 1983
ilver gelatine prints mounted on aluminium
x 210 mm each
by the artist

Hütte (Germany b.1951)
on, 1982-4
r gelatine print
x 400 mm
by Galerie Rudolf Kicken, Cologne

on, 1982-4
r gelatine print
x 400 mm
by Galerie Rudolf Kicken, Cologne

on, 1982-84
r gelatine print
x 500 mm
by Galerie Rudolf Kicken, Cologne

on, 1982-84
r gelatine print
x 500 mm
by Galerie Rudolf Kicken, Cologne

uhiro Ishimoto (Japan b.1921)
e-mat Room of the Music Suite, viewed from the south-

the Katsura Villa Series, 1981-2
transfer print
x 432 mm
by Photo Gallery International, Tokyo

ance Room of the Shoiken Pavilion, viewed from the
h Veranda. Middle Room beyond
the Katsura Villa Series, 1981-2
transfer print
x 432 mm
by Photo Gallery International, Tokyo

onoma in the Main Room of the Gepparo Pavillion, viewed
the south-east
the Katsura Villa Series, 1981-2
transfer print
x 432 mm
by Photo Gallery International, Tokyo

ms of Old Shoin, viewed from the east
the Katsura Villa Series, 1981-2
transfer print
x 432 mm
t by Photo Gallery International, Tokyo

Kamman (Netherlands 1898-1963)
Van Nelle Factory, 1929-30
er gelatine print (modern print)
 234 mm
t by the Van Nelle Factory Archive, Rotterdam

bara Kasten (USA)
hitectural Site 16, Whitney Museum of Art, 1987
achrome
4 x 1270 mm
t by John Weber Gallery, New York

Architectural Site 19, Pavillion for Japanese Art, L.A. County
Museum of Art, 1989
Cibachrome
1016 x 762 mm
Lent by John Weber Gallery, New York

Arthur Koster (Germany 1890-1965)
Einstein Tower, Potsdam, c. 1923
silver gelatine print (facsimile print produced by
Kunstbibliotek Staatliche Museen Preussischer Kulturbesitz,
Berlin)
228 x 156 mm

Werner Mantz (Germany 1901-1990)
Kölnische Zeitung, 1928
silver gelatine print
165 x 215 mm
Lent by the Board of Trustees of the Victoria and Albert
Museum, London

Stairwell, 1928
silver gelatine print
220 x 156 mm
Lent by the Board of Trustees of the Victoria and Albert
Museum, London

Gordon Matta-Clark (USA 1943-78)
Office Baroque, 1977
Cibachrome
1118 x 864 mm
Lent by Holly Solomon Gallery, New York

Joel Meyerowitz (USA b.1938)
St Louis and the Arch, 1978
colour print
406 x 508 mm
Lent by the artist

St Louis and the Arch, 1979
colour print
406 x 508 mm
Lent by the artist

Ryuji Miyamoto (Japan b.1947)
Asakusa Shochiku Movie Theatre, Tokyo, 1984
silver gelatine print
356 x 533 mm
Lent by the Simon Lowinsky Gallery, New York

Pavilion of Tsukuba Expo ' 85, Tsukuba, 1985
silver gelatine print
356 x 533 mm
Lent by the Simon Lowinsky Gallery, New York

Grosses Schauspielhaus, East Berlin, 1985
silver gelatine print
356 x 533 mm
Lent by the Simon Lowinsky Gallery, New York

Lucia Moholy (UK b.1894)
View from Vestibule Window to Laboratory Block, 1925/26
silver gelatine print (facsimile print produced by the Bauhaus
Archive, Berlin)
220 x 170 mm

Moholy-Nagy Dining-room, 1926
silver gelatine print (facsimile print produced by the Bauhaus
Archive, Berlin)
230 x 170 mm

László Moholy-Nagy (USA 1895-1946)
Berlin Radio Tower, 1925
silver gelatine print (facsimile print produced by the Bauhaus
Archive, Berlin)
236 x 175 mm

Dessau Building Balconies, 1927
silver gelatine print (facsimile print produced by the Bauhaus
Archive, Berlin)
393 x 294 mm

Beaumont Newhall (USA b.1908)
Chase National Bank, New York, 1928
silver gelatine print
260 x 259 mm
Lent by Scheinbaum and Russek Ltd, Santa Fe, New Mexico

Nicholas Nixon (USA b.1947)
View toward Midtown from Wall Street, New York, 1975
silver gelatine print
197 x 247 mm
Lent by a private collector

Martin Parr (UK b.1952)
Glencar, County Sligo, 1982
silver gelatine print
203 x 304 mm
Lent by the artist

Albert Renger-Patzsch (Germany 1897-1966)
Lubecker Blast Furnace, Winderhitzer, 1927
silver gelatine print
384 x 270 mm
Lent by the Museum Folkwang, Essen

Industrial Landscape, 1929
silver gelatine print
202 x 276 mm
Lent by the Museum Folkwang, Essen

Alexander Mikhailovich Rodchenko (USSR 1891-1956)
Mosselprom House, Moscow, 1926
silver gelatine print
152 x 228 mm
Lent by The Museum of Modern Art, Oxford

The Shukhov's Tower, 1927
silver gelatine print
96 x 146 mm
Lent by The Museum of Modern Art, Oxford

Thurman Rotan (USA b.1903)
Untitled, c.1932
silver gelatine print (facsimile print produced by the Art
Institute of Chicago; ref no : 1988.157.72)
114 x 222 mm

Georges Rousse (France b.1947)
Untitled, Marseille, 1986
cibachrome mounted on aluminium
1570 x 1000 mm
Lent by Musées de Marseille; courtesy of Galerie Farideh
Cadot, Paris

Sherrill V Schell (USA 1877-1964)
Brooklyn Bridge, 1930s
silver gelatine print (facsimile print produced by the Art
Institute of Chicago; ref no : 1988.157.75)
460 x 356 mm

Karl-Hugo Schmölz (Germany 1879-1938)
Hotel Disch AG, Cologne, 1929
silver gelatine print
172 x 157 mm
Lent by the Museum Folkwang, Essen

Catholic Church, Norderney, 1931
silver gelatine print
165 x 215 mm
Lent by the Museum Folkwang, Essen

Charles Sheeler (USA 1883-1965)
Industry (triptych, design for a mural) 1932
3 silver gelatine prints (facsimile prints produced by the Art
Institute of Chicago; ref no : 1975.1146 a-c)
200 x 382 mm

Julius Shulman (USA b.1910)
Raphael Soriano Arts and Architecture Case Study House, 1952
silver gelatine print
508 x 406 mm
Lent by the artist

Living Area of Pierre Koenig's Case Study House No. 22, 1960
silver gelatine print
508 x 406 mm
Lent by the artist

Eduard Steichen (USA 1879-1973)
The Flatiron Building, 1906
green, three-colour halftone, from 'Camera Work', April 1906
211 x 165 mm
Lent by The Royal Photographic Society, Bath

Otto Steinert (Germany 1915-78)
Rheinstahl Tower Block, Essen, 1961
silver gelatine print
358 x 593 mm
Lent by the Museum Folkwang, Essen

Ezra Stoller (USA b.1915)
S.C. Johnson Administration Building and Research Tower, 1944
silver gelatine print
356 x 279 mm
Lent by Esto Photographics, New York
© Esto

Solar Telescope, Kitt Peak, Arizona, 1962
silver gelatine print
356 x 279 mm
Lent by Esto Photographics, New York
© Esto

TWA Terminal, Idlewild (later J.F.Kennedy) Airport, New York, 1962
silver gelatine print
356 x 279 mm
Lent by Esto Photographics, New York
© Esto

Dulles International Airport Terminal Building, 1963
silver gelatine print
356 x 279 mm
Lent by Esto Photographics, New York
© Esto

Marine Midland Building, New York,1967
colour print
413 x 635 mm
Lent by Esto Photographics, New York
© Esto

Paul Strand (USA 1890-1976)
Wall Street, New York, 1915
platinum/palladium print, printed from the original negative by Richard Benson in 1976-77 at Paul Strand's direction
248 x 317 mm
Lent by the Paul Strand Foundation, Millerton, New York

Tim Street-Porter (UK b.1939)
Gehry Residence, 1981
silver gelatine print
268 x 176 mm
Lent by the artist

Santa Monica Place, 1982
silver gelatine print
176 x 267 mm
Lent by the artist

Orange County, 1985
silver gelatine print
205 x 261 mm
Lent by the artist

Bob Thall (USA b.1948)
Chicago, 1980
silver gelatine print
406 x 508 mm
Lent by the artist

Chicago, 1982
silver gelatine print
406 x 508 mm
Lent by the artist

Chicago, 1987
silver gelatine print
406 x 508 mm
Lent by the artist

Judith Turner (USA)
Michael Graves, Benacerraf House, 1979
platinum silver print
150 x 235 mm
Lent by the artist

Peter Eisenman House Thom loft, New York, 1989
platinum silver print
320 x 238 mm
Lent by the artist

Peter Eisenman House Thom loft, New York, 1989
platinum silver print
340 x 244 mm
Lent by the artist

Peter Eisenman House Thom loft, New York, 1989
platinum silver print
336 x 246 mm
Lent by the artist

Catherine Wagner (USA b. 1953)
Arch Construction III, George Moscone Site, San Francisco, 1981
silver gelatine print
364 x 472 mm
Lent by the artist
Eastern Vista, George Moscone Covention Center Site, San Francisco, 1981
silver gelatine print
363 x 465 mm
Lent by the artist

View from the Wonderwall, Louisiana World Exposition, New Orleans, 1984
silver gelatine print
368 x 470 mm
Lent by the artist

Garry Winogrand (USA 1928-84)
The Flatiron Building, New York City, 1974
silver gelatine print
322 x 222 mm
Lent by Centre Canadien d'Architecture/Canadian Centre Architecture, Montréal

Julia Wood (UK b.1953)
White Square, 1988
three from a series of six works (edition of 10)
gouache on silver gelatine print mounted on board
506 x 606 mm each
Lent by Actualites, London

Blue Dot No.2, 1991
a site-specific work by Julia Wood with Edward Woodman, specially commissioned by The Photographers' Gallery for the facade of Halina House during the exhibition
Cibachrome

Frank Rowland Yerbury (UK 1885-1970)
Midway Dancing Gardens, Chicago, 1913
silver gelatine print (modern print)
406 x 610 mm
Lent by the Architectural Association, London

Neuerberg Cigarette Factory, Hamburg, 1926
silver gelatine print (modern print)
610 x 406 mm
Lent by the Architectural Association, London

Anti-God Museum in St Isaac's Cathedral, Leningrad, 1932
silver gelatine print (modern print)
406 x 406 mm
Lent by the Architectural Association, London

Unknown
French Factory Interior, c.1890s
cyanotype
236 x 294 mm
Lent by Ken and Jenny Jacobson, Essex

Unknown
Berlin, Grosses Schauspielhaus, c.1920
facsimile print produced by the Technische Universität, Berlin
175 x 230 mm

ENDERS TO THE EXHIBITION

would like to express our gratitude to the
owing who have made this exhibition
ssible:-

tualites, London
aid, London
chitectural Association, London
chitectural Press, London
vo Barbieri, Italy
briele Basilico, Milan
ella Bayer, California
lène Binet, London
ya Brandt, London
tish Architectural Library Photographs
llection, London
ntre Canadien d'Architecture/Canadian
ntre for Architecture, Montréal
rtin Charles, London
icago Historical Society
liam Clift, Santa Fe
nn Davies, Wales
hn Donat, London
n Dow, Massachusetts
to Photographics, New York
lker Evans Estate, Connecticut
omann inc, New York
tmar Hörl, Frankfurt
n and Jenny Jacobson, Essex
non Lowinsky Gallery, New York

Marlborough Graphics, London
Joel Meyerowitz, New York
Musée Cantini, Marseille
Museum of Fine Arts, Houston
Museum Folkwang, Essen
Museum of Modern Art, Oxford
Pace/MacGill Gallery, New York
Martin Parr, Bristol
Photo Gallery International, Tokyo
Print Room, The Photographers' Gallery,
London,
Royal Photographic Society, Bath
Galerie Rudolf Kicken, Cologne
Scheinbaum and Russek Ltd, Santa Fe
Julius Shulman, Los Angeles
Holly Solomon Gallery, New York
Paul Strand Foundation, New York
Tim Street-Porter, Los Angeles
Syracuse University Library, New York
Chris Taylor, London
Bob Thall, Chicago
Judith Turner, New York
Van Nelle Factory Archive, Rotterdam
Victoria and Albert Museum, London
Waddington Graphics, London
Catherine Wagner, San Francisco
John Weber Gallery, New York
Mike Wells, London

NOTES ON CONTRIBUTORS

Martin Caiger-Smith is Exhibitions Organiser
at the Hayward Gallery, London

Robert Elwall is Curator of Photographs at
the British Architectural Library, Royal Institute
of British Architects, London

Ian Jeffrey is an art historian, writer and
curator who has written extensively on
photography. He is the author of *Photography:
A Concise History*, Thames and Hudson, 1981

Janet Abrams is Director of the Chicago
Institute for Architecture and Urbanism

Peter Greenaway is a film-maker, artist and
writer; his films include *The Draughtsman's
Contract, The Belly of An Architect* and *The
Cook, The Thief, His Wife and Her Lover.*